Your Healthy
CAT

Your Healthy
CAT

Homeopathic Medicines for Common Feline Ailments

H.G. Wolff, D.V.M.

North Atlantic Books
Berkeley, California

Homeopathic Educational Services
Berkeley, California

Your Healthy Cat:
Homeopathic Medicines for Common Feline Ailments

Copyright © 1991 by H.G. Wolff, D.V.M.
ISBN 1–55643–113–9

Published by
North Atlantic Books
2800 Woolsey Street
Berkeley, California 94705
and
Homeopathic Educational Services
2124 Kittredge Street
Berkeley, California 94704

Original edition published by Johannes Sonntag

Cover photograph by Richard Blair
Cover and book design by Paula Morrison

Printed in the United States of America

Your Healthy Cat: Homeopathic Medicines for Common Feline Ailments is sponsored by the Society for the Study of Native Arts and Sciences, a nonprofit educational corporation whose goals are to develop an educational and crosscultural perspective linking various scientific, social, and artistic fields; to nurture a holistic view of arts, sciences, humanities, and healing; and to publish and distribute literature on the relationship of mind, body, and nature.

Table of Contents

Foreword

Dear Cat-Owner,

Cats are loveable! At least that is the opinion of anyone who has the luck to own a cat. Precisely because cats are such independent personalities, it is a gratifying experience to win their affection. This also holds true when a cat tries hard not to show affection for her owner; after all, one should not reveal everything....

But a medium- to large-sized catastrophe occurs in the cat-owner's household when his four-legged purring pet falls ill. When the cat will not eat, her skin seems to hang from her bones, or when still more serious signs of illness manifest themselves, it is obvious that the cat is not well.

A cat can produce a wide variety of sounds, but she cannot make clear where it hurts, what she is lacking and how she is feeling. Therefore, human beings are frequently helpless when it comes to treating sick pets. In many cases, a trip to the veterinarian is the only sensible solution.

This is certainly often justified and better than letting the cat suffer or allowing her condition to worsen. However, there are various complaints that can be cured quickly and effectively by the cat-owner with relatively simple remedies. This book sets forth some of these remedies, along with advice on judging a cat's condition.

Dr. H.G. Wolff, Veterinarian
West Germany

Introduction

Why Homeopathy Helps Your Cat

Homeopathy was developed by Dr. Samuel Hahnemann for human patients. The first principle discovered by Dr. Hahnemann was that "each disease is most safely, quickly and comfortably cured by the remedy—in minute doses—which, given large doses, produces a reaction in the healthy body that most closely resembles the symptoms in question."

Hahnemann's first principle is as follows:

"May like to be cured by like."

Since Hahnemann made this truly revolutionary discovery more than 180 years ago, homeopathy has cured millions of people.

In the process, it was necessary to test the remedies on healthy people to discover their effect so they could subsequently be used to cure similar symptoms. Only in this way was it possible to make homeopathic remedies serviceable.

Hahnemann, his co-workers and successors have taken great pains to continue such thorough testing, so that today sick people all over the world may benefit. Maybe you have been helped by homeopathic medicine.

But how is it possible to apply homeopathic methods to pets?

The human being details the medical profile exactly during testing. Along with the primary symptoms, some subjec-

1

tive symptoms manifest themselves which an animal cannot describe.

Because there are universal laws of nature, it is possible and even predictable that some similar characteristic, objective, visible symptoms of human beings also appear in other animals. Since humans and animals display many of the same symptoms during testing, the results of medical tests on humans can often be transferred to cats. Animals can be cured with medications tested on humans—a happy circumstance for cat-owners since the conventional medications offered by the pharmaceutical industry have been tested on thousands of laboratory animals. Considering all the drug testing that animals must experience, it seems appropriate that the animal world can now enjoy the benefits of what animals have more than paid for.

If you proceed according to the homeopathic method of healing, it is necessary to administer the smallest possible potent dose since this will be sufficient to eliminate and cure the symptoms which resemble the remedy.

In other words: side-effects, an overdose of medication, a poisoning or other similar complications are unthinkable.

The field of homeopathic medicine is so large that only the most important principles can be introduced in this book. However, its contents are more than sufficient to keep a cat healthy.

At the beginning, a disorder should be treated without delay. If this occurs, the worst can often be avoided. This volume should not replace the veterinarian, but hopefully it can help the cat-owner provide first aid for his pet, much to his own satisfaction; after all, the health of our pets is an important part of our own health.

Maybe you have also heard from the wise men of our time that all of the undeniable successes of homeopathy are derived from autosuggestion. If the patient firmly believes that the medicine helps him, then maybe it really does help him.

But these wise men will quickly become confounded when you ask them how homeopathy can cure animals too. An animal, maybe a cat, is given a medicine about which it knows nothing. A substance, whose purpose is unknown to the animal, is mixed into its food and its illness and pain are alleviated.

Thus, one can no longer truly attribute homeopathy's success to the power of suggestion and autosuggestion. Quite often, in fact, when administering medication to animals, it must be done in such a way that they notice nothing, otherwise they will refuse it. Animals are cured by homeopathic remedies because these remedies are effective, not because of the power of suggestion.

Hahnemann, the founder of this "medicine of the future," made his discovery 180 years ago. Today it is still ahead of its time. Even for those people who have been cured by homeopathy, for those who are aware of its effects, it cannot be reconciled with contemporary canonical scientific knowledge. The natural sciences still cannot explain how the remedies work. This does not disturb people familiar with homeopathy, however, for they have witnessed millions of cures in the course of the decades. For the thankful patients, the true believers, this is already proof enough.

You should know this and take heart. Your cat will be treated with homeopathic remedies that can only help, and in no way hurt her.

Hahnemann says that only an inexperienced observer could believe "that animals cannot inform us just as well and precisely about their symptoms as human beings. They do not have a language, but the number of noticeable changes in their expressions, their behavior and their performance of natural, bestial and life-functions more than makes up for their lack of language. Since an animal knows nothing of play-acting, it does not exaggerate its pain, hide its feelings, or lie about complaints which are not there, as do human beings spoiled by education and morals who are sometimes inclined to alter their responses according to their moods. What becomes clear is that the symptoms an animal expresses present an honest picture of its inner condition and illness.

"Furthermore, animals are in our power. They must follow the diet we prescribe for them. They cannot lie to us or deceive us as human beings can when they have hidden symptoms about which the doctor knows nothing.

"Homeopathic methods for animals are, in a word, exactly as safe and sure as they are for human beings."

There then follows a paragraph which ensures Hahnemann's place in the company of early animal-rights advocates and puts him alongside his contemporary, Goethe. In an era in which many people would do anything to animals that he desired, Goethe says that "even the poor animals, who cannot exact justice from their tormentors, have earned the pity of the citizens of the world."

Goethe's first mention of the protection of animals was a passing remark:

> "Whosoever tortures animals has no soul,
> and the good spirit of God is not in him.
> Even should he look deep inside himself,
> one can never trust him."

This still holds true today, but unfortunately, much has changed since then.

Remedies

Homeopathy employs a variety of raw materials, including the following:

1) a. **mineral substances** such as gold, arsenic, mercury, and sulfur.

    b. **vegetable materials** such as *Belladonna* (deadly nightshade), *Allium cepa* (onion), and *Thuja* (tree of life).

    c. **animal substances** such as *Apis* (the honeybee), snake venoms such as *Lachesis* and *Crotalus*, or *Spongia* (deep sea sponges).

2) These substances are prepared according to homeopathic methods—by shaking and grinding into simultaneous potency and denaturation and mixing with a neutral base (water, alcohol, lactose). All kinds of animals love the lactose preparations, especially the tablets and triturations (powders).

3) The **Materia medica** documents the totality of symptoms discovered in pharmacological tests for all homeopathic remedies. It is constantly being expanded. In the human *materia medica* we find:

    a. **subjective symptoms** including changes in the psyche or moods, abnormal sensations, or pains. All of these symptoms are not available to the veterinarian. Therefore he must rely on the objective symptoms.

    b. **objective symptoms** such as thirst, vomiting, diarrhea, coughs, loss of hair, etc.

4) **Modalities**

    These are improvements or deteriorations due to movement, quiet rest, touch, the atmosphere, etc. They are important criteria upon which the choice between two related remedies may be made.

5) **Organ-Specific Remedies**
These have a specific curative effect on a particular organ.

IMPORTANT NOTE: There are numerous homeopathic medicines that are available and legal in Europe but not in the United States.

* next to the name of a medicine indicates that this substance is available only by prescription from a veterinary physician or another doctor who can legally prescribe drugs. (Medical doctors can prescribe these drugs in every state, and naturopathic physicians can prescribe them in approximately 10 states.)

** next to the name of a medicine indicates that this substance is not available at all to any licensed or unlicensed person in the U.S. A medicine is not legal here either because it has not been formally tested and accepted by the Homeopathic Pharmacopeia Convention of the United States, or because the original ingredient is an FDA-controlled substance, even in the homeopathic infinitesimal dose, as is the case with **Opium.**

Selection of a Remedy

In order to select the correct remedy, it is necessary to examine the patient and describe all symptoms he displays. Then one consults the *materia medica* to find the remedy which elicits similar symptoms.

This task is difficult and tiresome, especially at the beginning, because unfortunately homeopathy can be neither easily nor quickly learned.

The doctor—whether for the human or other animal—must invest much time and energy in familiarizing himself or herself with the remedies so that the appropriate remedy in any given case can be quickly discerned. You as a cat-owner and medical layman need not take such pains.

It is the purpose of this book to name the remedy most likely to cure each illness of your cat. Specialists speak of "proven indications," which in the majority of cases will provide reliable help. If you know these or learn them by reading about them, the work of homeopathic medicine is made easy.

If you wish to learn more about homeopathy, you will find sufficient resources in the list of references at the back of this book.

Potency

There are a variety of potencies created from the raw materials by grinding or, in the case of a tincture, by shaking. Through dilution and denaturizing comes the increasing strength of the remedy.

In general, **6** is the potency appropriate for home treatment.

Should another potency have proven effective in one case or another, it will be clearly indicated (e.g. **Berberis 3** or **Baptisia 3 or 30**). Otherwise, the potency for all homeopathic remedies discussed here is **6**. If you do not have the specific potency recommended and it is not immediately available, use the closest possible potency available to you.

Only after considerable experience can you be assured that you will make the right choice at a critical moment. It is best if you perform your first experiments with homeopathic treatment of cats in cases of very simple illnesses. You will soon see what the effects are and become more confident about the remedies and your ability to administer them.

This book provides information on how to treat simple conditions as well as life-threatening problems. The advice given is not meant to take the place of proper veterinary care, but to supplement it. Remember, although this book may prove to be invaluable to you and to your cat, you are not yet an expert when you have this book and use it to seek out remedies!

It may be that after you experience the favorable effects of these remedies upon your cat, you will decide homeopathy is the thing for you in case of illness. Perhaps you will look around to see whether you can find an appropriate doctor.

Maybe one day you will owe your health to the simple fact that you consulted this book in order to help your cat.

Dosage

In the beginning in cases of acute and rapidly developing illness, administer one dosage every hour approximately three to five times. Once improvement is noticeable, increase the interval between dosages—if necessary, administer three times a day during the ensuing days.

> One dosage
>> is 2–5 tablets
>> or 5–10 grains
>> or 5–10 drops
> according to the form of the remedy available to you.

The lactose base of the tablets, grains, or triturations (powders) tastes the best to a sick cat.

Drops should only be used in case of emergency since they contain alcohol. The size of the drops is not very important.

The main thing is that the organism absorbs the healing-stimulant. Mass and weight do not play as large a role as with chemical preparations, where the effects and side-effects (a nice paraphrase of poisoning!) are determined by the dosage.

So, while it may seem remarkable that the dosages are all the same for human beings, horses, dogs and cats, as well as seahorses and elephants, from the point of view of homeopathy this is understandable.

The increasing improvement is visible in the general condition: the cat feels better, relieved. She does not vomit or have any more diarrhea—if that was the problem. Often, she will take a nap directly after taking her medicine—this is a good omen for the correct choice of remedy.

Healing sleep must not always occur, however. With increasing improvement, it is not necessary to repeat the dosage. As soon as a normal condition is achieved, stop! Do not repeat the dosage "for safety's sake!" Homeopathy is an immunostimulating therapy, and that which is stimulated will continue without remedies.

If the illness is less acute, administer two to three dosages per day for several days. For chronic illnesses, continue administering the dosages over a longer period of time. If the treatment is with high potencies, there should be longer intervals between dosages, as you will learn in the following pages.

When purchasing homeopathic remedies, you will be amazed at the small sum the pharmacist asks for them—especially in comparison to the prices of drugs produced by the pharmaceutical industry. In the case of modern chemical preparations (most of which have not yet been on the market five years and will be replaced within the next five), production costs are high because of the unreasonably high cost of research and development. Research and development costs inevitably have an effect on the retail prices of the drugs. Homeopathic remedies are different: they do not go out of fashion and they last. People know how they work because of the careful research and testing performed free of charge by generations of homeopathic physicians. If the worth of this testing process were to be expressed in numbers, an additional zero would have to be added to the prices of all homeopathic remedies.

How to Administer Medicine to a Cat

The remedies work most quickly when they are absorbed through the mucous membranes of the mouth and enter directly into the bloodstream. Anyone who has a cooperative cat should crush a tablet between two spoons and apply the powder to the tongue with a damp fingertip. If necessary, put the remainder of the remedy on the cat's front paws; she will consume it the next time she cleans herself. Because all tablets or powders (triturations) taste like lactose, it is no problem to get the remedies into cooperative cats.

In exceptional cases when it is not possible to administer the remedy in the manner indicated above, stir the tablet into milk or drinking water. Another method is to put the crushed tablet into ground meat or any other favorite food. But remember not to feed the cat too much at one time; it must be done often.

In the pharmacy, it is important to insist that the remedy be in tablet form. It is also possible to obtain remedies in liquid form, dissolved in alcohol, but this does not taste as good to the cat as do tablets with the lactose base.

Tinctures, such as **Calendula** (marigold) or **Euphrasia** (eye-bright), which are recommended for eye inflammations and conjunctivitis, should never be put into the eye undiluted. The degree of dilution for eye-baths should be one drop per teaspoonful boiled water. If this is still too strong (as is the case for some cats), dilute the tincture still further. Only one exception applies for cats: in the case of inflammation of the ear canal, put drops of undiluted Calendula tincture directly into the ear. Be careful that when the cat shakes her head after the ears have been massaged, none of the undiluted tincture gets into the eyes.

Storage of the Homeopathic Remedies

Your homeopathic home pharmacy should be stored in a special corner far from sunlight, heat, strong perfumes, disinfecting agents, or similar substances. If thus stored, the remedies keep for a long time, even your lifetime.

There are doctor-families in Germany and Switzerland in their third or fourth generation as homeopaths who still have remedies prepared by their grandfathers and great-grandfathers (in those days, doctors dispensed remedies themselves, as veterinarians and a small group of doctors still do). These remedies are still used today and have proven to be just as effective now as ever.

Normal Body Function

The normal body functions of the healthy cat are:

- 20–25 breaths per minute
- Body temperature up to 103 degrees Fahrenheit
- Pulse rate between 110–170

Sweat is only possible on the paw-pads. Cats sweat when they are frightened or ill. They also sometimes sweat when they are excited, as they tend to be when they are exhibited at cat shows.

Shedding occurs in spring and fall. The true luster of the fur comes with maturity, at approximately six months to 30 months.

Intake of food is not the same as for the dog, a pack-animal. The cat is an individualist. Solitary hunters in the wild, cats seek out a place and claim their food. Parts of the catch are torn off and swallowed. The healthy stomach can tolerate relatively large quantities. The prickly tongue serves primarily as a tool to maintain the fur and take in liquids. As with all carnivores, the intestine is short, the stomach is capable of much distension, and the gastric juices are sharp.

The body-language of cats is easy to translate:

- if a cat wants to attract attention, she will rub herself against a person's legs or against the furniture with her tail sticking straight up;

- a sharply angled tail indicates she is feeling good;

- a slow, sweeping beat with the tail indicates no enmity, and affection is growing;

- if the end of the tail vibrates, it indicates the cat is distrustful and will not put up with everything;

- the beating of the entire tail indicates anger and pain, a state of excitement;

- an arched back shows readiness to fight. In this case, the ears are also flattened back.

Whomever wishes to examine, treat, brush, or do anything else to a cat does well to stroke her with both hands in rapid succession on the back of the head or to massage her gently (but without wearing rings!). This quiets and reassures her and alleviates her fear. As any veterinarian will tell you, she will even tolerate an injection without a fight.

A Word about Character and Behavior

There is an amusing comparison between the nature of cats and dogs. The dog, it is said, is an employee; the cat, in contrast, is an independent co-worker. In this there is a lot of truth. A cat will not take orders. She hears her name and knows that it refers to her, but will not come immediately when called. In principle, she only comes when it pleases her to do so. You cannot force cats to do anything. They conduct themselves as they wish and do not allow themselves to be "trained" (The exception here are cats who are specifically raised for the show ring. If training begins shortly after birth, it is possible to train cats to pose, behave, greet strangers, and perform.).

While the owner is the "master" to a dog, that is to say his "benevolent God," the owner plays second fiddle to the cat. Most cats believe people are only there to serve them. It takes a lot of trouble, emotional investment, tender care, and understanding to form a bond with a cat. The cat then decides on her own to become attached to and share her affection with her owner. However, when a cat has had bad experiences with people (especially at a young age), this is programmed into her brain and she will never forget it. She will remain shy and scared, aloof and prone to scratch, and a person may not understand where the root of the problem lies. Some cats are indelibly marked by such a psychological disturbance.

It is an old belief—which often proves correct—that a cat is more attached to her house or apartment than to any particular person. Therefore, it matters far less to a cat than to a dog when she is left alone at home during family vacations and is looked after by a friend. As long as the friend sees to it that the cat is fed one or two times a day and the litter box is kept clean (in this case, two litter boxes are advisable), the cat is satisfied. She is in familiar surroundings and does not need to readjust.

Undoubtedly there are also cats that can easily be taken on trips, but this prospect is risky since cats become agitated in new surroundings. In rare cases, a cat may even run away because she is disturbed by unfamiliar surroundings.

Cats are hard-nosed about their desires. When a cat you have banned from the kitchen or another room gets it into her head that she wants to be in just that room, she will not tire of trying to get in. You can be quite certain that she will do it. And in the end, you will give in before the cat will. But it is precisely such characteristics that are expressions of the individualistic personality which make each cat—*your* cat— loveable! You probably agree.

The purpose of this book is to suggest remedies which anyone can easily use to help his cat in times of sickness and health. These remedies can only help your cat, not hurt her.

I, a veterinarian, have written this book because I love these magical creatures just as you do, and because I believe that thanks to homeopathic remedies, you too can stand by your cat in her illness as you never before thought possible.

With this advice, my hope is that your cat becomes and stays healthy!

When is a Cat Sick?

The first thing the cat-owner will notice is that the cat behaves differently than usual. She may:

- lie apathetically where she normally plays,
- refuse her usual food,
- seek out your company, but only reluctantly allow you to touch her,
- run constantly to the litter box,
- her eyes may tear or she sneezes or is plagued by diarrhea,

then it is time to pay some intensive attention to your cat!!

1

Eyes, Ears, and Mouth

Eyes

Luckily, cats' eyes are generally quite healthy, and serious eye diseases are a rarity. Surgical intervention in cases of deformation of the eyelid, inversion of the eyelid (Entropion), growths on the cornea, tumors of the eyelid, or even prolapse of the eyeball are the domain of the experienced veterinarian. What happens more frequently are wounds and inflammations caused by cat fights. They are not very difficult to treat.

Injuries, Inner Eyelid

Injuries in the vicinity of the eye, eyelid, or cheek, which are often the result of battles between tomcats, are best treated with a **Calendula** bath. Put twenty drops of the tincture into one cup of warm water. Moisten the wound with a cotton ball three or four times each day for several days.

Internally, one tablet of the homeopathic remedy **Hepar sulphuris 12** can be administered three times a day until healing sets in.

17

Like the dog, the cat also has an inner, or third, eyelid. It serves to protect the eyeball and can cover nearly the entire surface like a membrane. It is particularly useful when the cat is crawling through fields where grass or grass pollen could get into her eyes. If the third eyelid comes down, it is lamed, and this indicates illness. You must not overlook this symptom and should take the cat to the veterinarian.

The conjunctiva, which when healthy should be nearly invisible, functions as a mucous membrane surrounding the eye.

Possible causes of conjunctivitis are dust or grass pollen in the eye, or drafts, such as those in a moving car with an open window. The conjunctiva can be injured by these things, bacteria can develop, and so the inflammation begins. Should the inflammation occur on just one side, the most likely culprit is a foreign body, perhaps grass pollen or chaff. Take the cat to the veterinarian immediately.

Conjunctivitis

Acute conjunctivitis will quickly be cured with eyedrops containing antibiotics. Should conjunctivitis recur or become complicated, however, a homeopathic examination and medicine is necessary. The following remedies may be used according to symptoms.

Euphrasia 3 (eye-bright). Discharge from the eyes is thick and irritating. Light-sensitive, swollen conjunctiva, often accompanied by sniffles and mild discharge from the nose.

Allium cepa 3 (onion) tears are noticeably hot but mild, not irritating—the consequence of colds or drafts. When accompanied by sniffles, then also by heavy discharge from the nose, which irritates the nostrils. These accompanying symptoms (sniffles and/or coughs) improve outdoors, but become worse in warm places. Watch if when your cat comes in from outdoors, to see if she feels worse.

Pulsatilla 4 (windflower). If the discharge from the eyes turns into yellowish-green pus two to five days after the onset of the illness (or if you first notice the cat's illness at this stage), then **Pulsatilla 4** is the remedy. The eyelids are red and swollen, but the area around the eye is not inflamed. Neither coughs nor sniffles are noticeable.

Natrum muriaticum 12 (salt). Indicated in cases of chronic discharge from the eyes and also for the completely normal eye. Here, the eye functions as a vent—harmful substances are discharged through the mucous membranes of the eye. In most such cases, dry food is the culprit—it should be replaced with fresh food. Other symptoms often present are the loss of hair, anxiety, and the fear of being touched. These symptoms will disappear along with the discharge from the eyes.

Cats that are permitted to go outside sometimes return with both an inflammation of the eyelids and conjunctivitis (Blepharoconjunctivitis). Slimy, pus-like secretions flow heavily. The eyes are closed, and underneath, the cornea is covered with blisters and abscesses. In this case, the patient is well provided for with the following remedy:

Mercurius solubilis 6 (mercury), which should be administered three times a day until the eyes are healthy and all signs of swelling have vanished. **Mercurius** renews the mucous membrane. The simultaneous application of an antibiotic salve to the eyes is recommended for several days.

Tear Ducts

A cat's tears flow from the inner corner of the eye through the tear duct into the nose. If the duct is blocked by a lameness of the inner eyelid, a particle of dust, or a growth, the tears run along the outside of the nose, leaving a brown trail behind them.

Successful treatment can be achieved with **Silicea 12** administered three times a day in the first week, then twice a day until the symptoms are cured.

Inflammation of the Cornea (Keratitis)

Sometimes when an indoor cat ventures into the great outdoors for the first time, the cornea—the transparent front part of the eyeball—can be injured by grass or bushes.

Such infections can also be caused by wounds received in fights, severe conjunctivitis, infection with the herpes virus, or a lack of Vitamin A. The cornea appears bluish-white and cloudy, and abscesses sometimes occur on the cornea itself. The cat can scarcely see anything if both eyeballs are involved. She is likely to sit alone in a corner, and because she is extremely sensitive, she will hardly allow herself to be examined. She definitely belongs in the hands of a veterinarian.

Hepar sulphuris 6 is the remedy at the beginning. After several days, when the cat will allow you to touch her and open her eyes, this remedy should be replaced with three daily dosages of **Mercuris corrosivus**. The cornea is among those tissues that regenerate themselves very slowly. Therefore, a cure takes time—you can count on weeks.

If scars remain on the cornea after the illness has subsided, administer **Conium 6**, and if traces still remain, **Calcarea carbonica 6**, each for ten days.

Glaucoma

Glaucoma refers to an increase in pressure on the eyeball, which can occur on one or both sides. The eyeball becomes enlarged due to the increased pressure. This condition does not cause the cat particular pain, and luckily, glaucoma is less common in cats than in dogs. At the beginning, it can be treated effectively with five drops of **Phosphorus 200** administered mornings and evenings for eight days (a proven remedy of the English veterinarian MacLeod).

Good results are also obtained with one dosage of **Belladonna 30** administered once a day for approximately ten days, but this only holds true if treatment is begun without delay. If the pressure inside the eye continues to increase, the eyeball becomes enlarged, and when it has reached a critical point the cat suffers severe pain, and blindness can result.

Cataracts

A cat's eye is subject to cataracts. In general, cataracts are a disease of old age. If cataracts occur at a young age, the culprit is most likely the cat's food. A change of diet should be instituted, accompanied by treatment with **Natrum muriaticum 12**. Administer one tablet twice a day for three weeks and repeat after four weeks if necessary. The change of diet is very important. The cat does not need a complicated diet, just another type of food.

The "normal" cataracts, which occur after a cat is about ten years old, require treatment with **Silicea**: administer **Silicea 12** twice a day for three weeks and then **Calcarea fluorica 12** twice a day for the same period of time. Wait four weeks, then repeat if necessary.

Ears

Healthy cats have healthy ears which do not need to be cleaned. If cleaning should become necessary, put a few drops of baby oil into the ears and massage them.

Inflammation of the Ear Canal

Inflammation of the ear canal is not difficult to recognize; an afflicted cat shakes her head and scratches herself behind the ears at every opportunity.

A grayish-white coating, often the result of ear mites, can lead to an accumulation of dark ear wax at the onset of an inflammation. A wad can form and plug up the ear canal, severely disturbing the behavior of the cat.

The desire to scratch increases evenings and in warm places. Clean the ear with a washcloth and your finger, and under a magnifying glass you can see the ear mites crawling. The eggs that they lay in the skin of the ear canal hatch into larvae after two days, which means that you must extend treatment over at least seven days.

Unfortunately, ear mites have another bad quality; they are contagious. If you discover ear mites in a cat that lives together with other cats or dogs, then all of the animals should be treated simultaneously.

Entire litters suffer from these ear mites when their presence has been overlooked in the mother.

A severe infestation in young animals can have serious consequences: the inflammation can cause changes in the inner ear which result in problems with balance, chronic tilting of the head, or even nervous problems (blindness, cramp-attacks, convulsions, weight loss, death).

In every case, a fast-acting remedy is called for: a few drops of full-strength **Calendula** tincture should be put into the ears once or twice a day. Massage the ears after pouring the drops in. Internally, **Calendula 3**, administered three times a day, is recommended. In this manner, the problem is solved quickly, gently, and without chemicals.

The situation is a bit different in the case of chronic inflammations. Here are a variety of other possibilities:

Graphites 6: The abundant ear wax has the look and consistency of honey. Often, you will notice eczema on the lips and eyes. These patients are robust, eat a lot, catch cold easily, and are frequently constipated.

Mercurius solubilis 6: This inflammation of the ear canal lasts a long time. It is accompanied by an intense desire to scratch and inflamed, swollen ear canals with thick crusts and yellow pus.

Petroleum 6: fissures and cracks in the ear indicate the need for this remedy. Dry eczema.

Hepar sulphuris 6: Because she is extremely sensitive around the ears, the cat will not let anyone near her. The discharge is yellowish and bloody, thick, and smells like old cheese. In this case, do not treat the area, but instead administer one tablet four times a day until the sensitivity decreases. You can then handle the cat and remove the pus and ear wax.

Psorinum 15: The discharge smells like cooked meat; yellowbrownish pus; the inflammation can last for years(!) and will only improve if you administer **Psorinum 15** twice a day. This patient is often cold, greedy, and she stinks. The symptoms, including the desire to scratch, are worse in winter. If the inflammation disappears by itself, symptoms often appear in the lungs and bronchial tubes.

Sulphur 6: Useful for the treatment of every otitis, as it ensures the infection does not reassert itself.

Inflammation of the Inner Ear

Seldom does an inflammation of the ear canal turn into an inflammation of the inner ear. A cat with an inner ear inflammation runs unsteadily in circles and is visibly disturbed.

Instead of administering massive doses of antibiotics and opening the eardrum, **Pulsatilla 200** is effective. Administer one dosage mornings and evenings for two days and wait to see what happens.

In the past this remedy has been sufficient first to improve the general condition of the patient, and then subsequently to cure local symptoms.

Hematoma

This is the common name for the discharge of blood between the skin and cartilage of the ear. Hematoma is characterized by a pillow-like, fluctuating curvature of the skin and by the way the cat continuously shakes her head.

Old, gray cats who are veterans of territorial battles and the associated tangles with dogs or other cats often suffer from hematoma. It is not particularly painful, but merely uncomfortable for the cat. She timidly scratches her ear, thus informing her owner of her condition. Before you consider surgical intervention by a veterinarian, however (not before three weeks have gone by), try to encourage the reabsorption of blood in order to decrease the swelling. The recommended remedy for this is **Arnica**.

Arnica 30 should be administered four times a day for three days in tablet form. In addition, massage the ear with **Arnica** gel or oil several times a day, or at the very least, mornings and evenings. From the fourth day on, use **Arnica 30** only two times a day until the discharge disappears, a process which can take between eight and twenty-one days, according to the age and condition of the cat. After twenty-one days if the cat has not shown marked improvement, consult your veterinarian.

Experience has shown that an operation is seldom necessary—in most cases, the blood is successfully reabsorbed. In old animals it is possible that the afflicted ear will remain a bit lopsided or thick, but in the second half of life, health comes before beauty.

Should an operation become necessary, then, as always before surgery: **Arnica 30** twice a day for two days beforehand and three times a day for three days after the operation (or **Arnica 6** four times a day). This promotes rapid, nearly painless healing and prevents hemorrhages and the formation of fistules.

Ear mites or infection can also cause a hematoma. See the sections on "Inflammation of the ear canal" and "Inflammation of the inner ear" for possible remedies.

Abscess of the Outer Ear

This condition is usually due to fungal infections but may also be caused by an inflammation of the ear canal or scratch wounds. Because of the constant shaking and scratching, it can be difficult to cure. The ear muscle really should be immobilized with a bandage and treated with **Hypericum tincture, Calendula tincture**, or another healing salve.

Hypericum is the oil of the herb St. John's wort, which relieves pain and attacks bacteria and fungi present in open portions of the wound. The tincture should be rubbed sparingly into the afflicted area twice a day. If the cat cleans herself and licks up the tincture, it will also work internally and be well-tolerated. This is not a surprise, considering the number of different ways to administer internal medicine to human beings.

You should always keep a supply of external applications of **Hypericum** at home, and if possible, prepare **Hypericum** oil yourself.

If you crush a piece of St. John's wort between your fingers, they will turn red. You should pick the blossoms and add three to four parts olive oil to them. Let this mixture stand four to six weeks in the sun or in a warm place, and then pour the red-tinted oil through a handkerchief. Then you will always have an outstanding natural healing remedy in the house which you can use not only for your cat, but also for your family. The oil retains its healing powers for at least two years.

Internally, the cat should be given one tablet of **Silicea** 12 two or three times a day until she is well. **Silicea**, silicic acid, works nicely as a specific remedy even when it must be administered over a longer period of time. It is simply without equal. If the cat scratches and her scratching causes wounds around the thickened area, an effective remedy is Silicea 30 administered three times a day for four to seven days. This should bring relief and cause the material under the skin to dissolve. If necessary, continue treatment for three more days.

Treatment with **Silicea 30** is valuable for all sorts of swellings of the skin. Such swellings are often considered impossible to cure, but it can be done!

Silicea, and only **Silicea 30**, is the appropriate remedy. Just think how much richer medicine would be if only people at universities would concern themselves with homeopathy!

Mouth (Oral Cavity)

Teeth

The young cat loses her twenty-six baby teeth within the first six months of her life, and as an adult, has thirty teeth by the time she is twelve months old.

You can do young cats a big favor by giving them **Calcarea phosphoricum**. If a cat receives **Calcarea phosphoricum** while she is teething, the result will be splendid teeth. Ideally, you should administer **Calcarea phosphoricum** from the fourth month on. Use one packet (10 g) of this remedy as a starting point for the development of healthy permanent teeth. This chance comes just once in a cat's lifetime—only during the time she is teething.

Later in their lives, cats are not spared dental problems.

Loose Teeth

Healthy but loose teeth that cause no pain can be treated with **Symphytum 3**. This will make the teeth hold fast again and help preserve them for a while longer. **Symphytum 3** must be added to the food at least twice a day for three weeks.

Teeth that are loose and painful are caused by damaged roots and therefore have no chance, just like teeth whose suppurated roots form fistules. They must be removed.

Tartar

Tartar formation is not a local problem, but rather has to do with a disturbance of the intermediary metabolism, which causes calcium salts to enter the saliva. The result of such a disturbance is tartar.

The degree of hardness and composition of the tartar are different in every organism. There is no homeopathic remedy.

If tartar develops in old age, it is recommended that your veterinarian remove it periodically with ultrasound. In extreme cases, the cat will have mouth odor because entire colonies of bacteria live on the tartar deposits. Swelling can even occur if the tartar constantly irritates the mucous membranes of the mouth.

If just a little tartar accumulates on the canine teeth, a simple remedy can help: baking soda. Use a damp washcloth to rub the tartar off the teeth. This approach has the advantage that if the baking soda is swallowed, it is easily tolerated.

Toothpastes containing baking soda are available in many pet shops.

Pockets in the Gums

Pockets in the gums are caused by tartar buildup. They form a reservoir for the primary causes of bad breath—food particles and germs. In addition, like teeth with "lazy" roots, they can cause problems in other organs, e.g. in the kidneys or heart, and they therefore must be treated. **Arnica 30** is recommended.

Swelling of the Gums (Epulis)

Swelling of the gums occurs not only in dogs, but in cats too. If the swelling spreads from the mucous membrane, **Thuja** is recommended. If the periosteum, the hard palate, is the starting point, **Symphytum** will help, and if the new growth begins from the bones, **Calcarea fluorica** is the appropriate remedy.

The distinction should be made on the basis of the different degrees of hardness of the tissues:

> soft—**Thuja**
> solid—**Symphytum**
> hard—**Calcarea fluorica**

The treatment should relieve the swelling.

It is also possible that the surgical removal of tissue for testing purposes can determine the choice of remedy. Eventually, epulis may consist of more than one swelling of the tissues. If this is the case, remedies must be selected individually.

The treatment lasts a long time and must be repeated twice a day in order to prevent a recurrence of the problem.

Cleft Palate
The natural splitting of the gums is an inherited trait and should not be treated, as it will only become worse.

The illness profile of an open split in the gums is typically that food taken into the mouth flows directly out through the nose after it has been swallowed. The cat must then sneeze. The actual slit in the gums is hardly noticeable.

Inflammation of the Gums (Gingivitis)
The digestive process begins in the oral cavity. Therefore, the oral cavity is the starting point of some illnesses in cats. It often happens that from birth, a cat has a reddish gum that does not hurt, but resists all kinds of treatment. If this reddish gum emits a bad odor, then it should be treated with **Kreosotum**.

This type of inflammation of the gums (gingivitis) not only stinks, but it can cause the secretion of irritating fluids and the bleeding of the mucous membranes. In extreme cases, the separation of the lip from the jaw causes severe pain and will only unwillingly be tolerated—if at all.

The inflammation subsides somewhat more quickly if the bacterial fields on the mucous membrane are "washed away" with antibiotics for a few days—but you don't have to do this!

If you give antibiotics to the cat the inflammation will subside, but according to experience, it will return once the medication has been stopped. This happens because the antibiotics fight only the accompanying bacteria—the mucous membranes are not cleaned as effectively as they are by **Kreosotum.**

Other remedies which complement the homeopathic remedies are rinses with sage tea from a disposable syringe (10 ml without a drainage tube), or the proven combination of

> **Arnica tincture*** (3x is an over-the-counter remedy)
> **Calendula tincture**
> **Myrrh tincture**
> in equal parts

Use one teaspoonful in one glass of warm water to rinse out the oral cavity.

One further helpful remedy for inflamed, swollen gum tissues that bleed easily, where the saliva flows and the glands —the parotid gland as well as the lymph nodes in the jaw— are swollen, is **Mercuris solubilis 6.** If you look closely, you will discover that the tongue has a grayish-white coating and is swollen. The cat may also suffer from diarrhea and be more thirsty than usual.

Another type of gum inflammation may be cured with one tablet of **Nitric acid 6** administered three times a day. In the case of this type of inflammation, the sore portion of the mouth and foul odor are noticeable; the entire oral cavity is affected, not just the gums, is affected, and the saliva, which may be bloody, is abundant. You will notice the cat experiences pain when swallowing, and each bite is painful, not only in the oral cavity when she chews, but also when she swallows (One further observation: the urine smells bad and defecation is painful.)

With these remedies you have a handle on inflammations of the gums and the accompanying inflammation of the mucous membranes of the mouth—unless your cat is suffering from a form of feline distemper in the course of which a severe inflammation of the mucous membranes of the mouth may occur.

Here, the obvious sign is the red, abscessed, and swollen rim of the tongue, which makes it impossible for the cat to consume food. This is a dark moment in the life of a cat-owner: the apathetic and feeble cat sits drooling in front of her food dish. She would very much like to eat, but she cannot.

If this should happen to your cat, consider treatment with **Baptisia** (wild indigo). In this illness profile, a sudden fever is accompanied by rapid exhaustion and lethargy. Also present is the penetratingly foul odor of the whole cat, and especially of the oral cavity, including the swollen rim of the tongue. The cat will not be able to eat or drink.

In veterinary practice it is frequently the case that a cat-owner does not believe his cat suffered from the feared feline distemper since the cure was so quick and effective. It should be noted that a cat cured of feline distemper need not be immunized against it; through exposure to the disease, cats develop a lifelong immunity to it.

A cure with **Baptisia** for this form of feline distemper is sure, quick, mild, and comfortable for the patient—it doesn't make a difference which potency you use. In an acute case, all dosages—3, 6, 12, or 30—are effective. Baptisia often makes antibiotics, steroids, heart and circulatory remedies, and dextrose infusions unnecessary.

With this example you can see exactly why the Indian government supports homeopathy: because homeopathy is easy, mild, non-violent, and above all, affordable! It is thus not surprising that that Mahatma Gandhi once said, "Homeopathy is the latest and refined method of treating patients economically and non-violently. Government must encourage and patronize it in our country."

Inflammation of the Mucous Membranes of the Mouth (Stomatitis)

An inflammation of the mucous membranes of the mouth occurs when an inflammation of the gums spreads.

This kind of inflammation is frequently caused by bone splinters, fish bones, needles, mold on grass consumed by the cat, the licking-up of sharp substances, etc.

A newly discovered, acute inflammation of the mucous membranes of the mouth calls for **Belladonna 4** along with **Echinacea 1**.

As a follow-up (if necessary after several days have elapsed), the remedy **Mercurius solubilis** is appropriate for the third stage (the first stage is the short **Aconitum** phase, then comes **Belladonna**, and then **Mercurius**). If grasses or chaff are the cause and these might have brought fungi into the inflamed area, **Mercurius** should be the administered.

Tongue Cyst (Ranula)

Ranula refers to a cyst under the tongue which is caused by the blockage of a salivary gland. When such a cyst reaches a certain size, it can interfere with the intake of food. The veterinarian makes an incision which creates a passage from the salivary gland into the oral cavity, thus relieving the cat's suffering, but not curing her.

Doses of **Thuja** are most effective if administered as soon as the swelling is observed. **Thuja** cures this complaint very nicely, as it cures similar complaints in dogs and human beings, by removing any blockages in the salivary gland.

Ulceration of the Lips (Eosinophiles Granulom)

Ulceration of the lips is another skin disease (often difficult to cure) which calls for **Silicea**. The eosinophile granulom appears mostly on the edge of the upper lip but can appear on the lower lip as well. Eosinophile granulom is also commonly experienced on the hamstring area of the rear legs, a condition called rodent ulcer.

It takes the form of an irritated, reddish wound and can, in extreme cases, look quite ghastly.

After a dosage of **Silicea 30** three times a day for seven days, you should switch to **Calcarea fluorica 30** from the tenth day on and administer this once a day until healing sets in—but do this at most for twenty-one days. Then wait four weeks and repeat if necessary.

Foreign Bodies in the Oral Cavity

In play or through food, foreign bodies such as bones, bone splinters, hangnails, or needles (with or without thread) can enter the oral cavity.

Needles swallowed without thread may pass harmlessly through the intestines dull end first and exit the body. Needles swallowed with thread present more of a problem.

A foreign body lodged in the oral cavity makes it presence known if the cat drools, vomits, or chokes.

First Aid before the visit to the vet: Wrap the cat in a blanket so that only her head shows, then try to remove the foreign body.

If a smallish bone is already lodged deeper, try feeding the cat softened bread together with chopped meat. Otherwise, take her directly to the veterinarian.

Somebody once brought me a cat that had been eating only with reluctance for six weeks. I removed (unbelievable as it might seem) a 5½ cm-long rusty sewing needle with thread from the right side of her throat—without an anesthetic. Today, this cat's picture is in one of the photo albums in my waiting room. I could neither treat the wound nor give her an injection (even though the oral cavity was severely inflamed) simply because her owner rushed out of my office so she could feed the cat. (This really happened!) I only saw the cat after another week had gone by: everything was fine, no further trace of inflammation to be seen—without any remedy!

This case clearly demonstrates the healing effects of nature, especially in the oral cavity, where the saliva of an otherwise healthy cat functions as an effective disinfectant.

2

Respiratory Tract

Nose

Colds

When an alert cat-owner who is familiar with colds in cats hears a cat sneeze, he recognizes that this could indicate a cold. If the cat then sneezes several more times, it is high time for a dosage of **Aconitum**.

Aconitum 6: The first remedy for acute feverish inflammations to be administered at the first sign of inflammation. The phase of an illness in which **Aconitum** can help is short and stormy. A few timely doses of **Aconitum** are sufficient not only to stop the cold, but also to cure it. **Aconitum** arrests the further development of the cold.

If the inflammation has already taken hold, then **Belladonna 4–6** is the remedy for the second phase. At the beginning, the cold—caused by catching cold, changes in the weather or infection from sick animals or people—causes the cat to sneeze and scrub and scratch at her nose. Later, the watery discharge becomes slimy or slimy/purulent, and the nostrils swell up and make breathing difficult. This condition calls for the use of the following remedy:

Lachesis 12. At this point it is sometimes possible to see an inflammation of the tonsils or a swelling of the lymph nodes at the edge of the lower jaw. Lachesis 12 should be administered three times a day for three or four days.

If no discharge occurs and the nostrils are so stopped up that the cat cannot breathe except through her mouth and if she sniffles and rasps, then one should use **Hepar sulphuris 12.** Should the cure not be complete, we recommend **Luffa 12.** Alternation between heavy discharge and the standstill of secretion is typical at this stage.

Other remedies for cats with colds are:

Allium cepa 3: Abundant, watery discharge irritates the nostrils and lips. Symptoms are worse in warm places and improve outdoors and in the cold.

Pulsatilla 4: Thick, yellow-slimy discharge, sometimes greenish, but mild, not irritating; flows in great quantities from both nostrils.

Most kinds of colds react well when given routine treatment: three days of **Lachesis**, then three days of **Hepar sulphuris**, both in the 12th potency.

Often, an old home remedy from grandmother's time is effective: the inhalation of chamomile vapors. The patient sits on a chair, the seat of which is made of tubes or slats. She is covered with a basket under which a pot of hot chamomile tea is placed. A sick cat should inhale the vapors for ten minutes a day.

Indeed, colds are not easy to cure, but the alteration of the mucous membranes, the cleansing of the "terrain," is more effective than the attack on accompanying bacteria with antibiotics. Once these conventional medications have been stopped, the cold usually returns. A complete cure happens rarely and takes a long time.

Therefore, be patient and careful when you select a remedy.

For animal homes in which such colds are common and eradication is difficult, try the following: to strengthen their immune reactions, all cats should be given **Echinacea 1** in their drinking water, and then three days of **Lachesis 30**, three days of **Hepar sulphuris 30**, and finally, three days of **Silicea 30** (also in the drinking water). Stir three tablets into one liter of drinking water and administer to all cats.

From the point of view of homeopathy it is not important that all of the water be consumed; the important thing is that the appropriate remedy is in the water, whether some remains in the evening or not.

Growths in the Nasal Passage

Occasionally, growths occur on the mucous membranes and appear in the nasal passages as polyps. Such growths make their presence known if they interfere with the cat's breathing. The nasal passages are obstructed, and snorting noises and a slimy-watery discharge from the nose are the result.

The remedy is **Thuja**, three dosages a day for two to three weeks. This has helped many cats, although **Teucrium marcum 1** is another possibility. **Teucrium marcum**—cat thyme —is appropriate when the cat sneezes a lot and the discharge is bloody.

Inflammation of the Sinuses (Sinusitis)

If a cold is not eradicated quickly, it can turn into sinusitis, the inflammation of the nose and nasal passages.

Discharge from one side of the nose is a symptom of sinusitis. Classification of the discharge indicates which remedy should be employed:

Hydrastis 6: thick, yellow, sometimes bloody discharge.

Cinnabaris 6: chronic sniffles with pus-like, slimy, yellowish-green discharge that smells bad.

Sticta pulmonaria 6: thick yellow discharge that does not smell bad, accompanied by a cough.

Phosphorus 12: in cases of chronic sinusitis, administer one to two times daily.

Throat

Inflammation of the Tonsils (Tonsillitis)

Like a human, a cat has two tonsils, one on the left and the other on the right side of the throat. The tonsils serve as "sentries" which intercept germs entering through the mouth and nose. Inflammation of the tonsils triggers a defensive reaction in the body. A proven remedy, which can also be used for people, is **Belladonna 4**, the remedy for local inflammation. Place one crushed tablet on the tongue every two hours. Should the tonsils remain thick after the inflammation has subsided, **Calcarea iodatum**, administered two to three times a day for several days, is effective.

Inflammation of the Throat (Pharyngitis)

If the inflammation spreads to the mucous membranes of the throat due to a viral infection, this is called pharyngitis. This condition causes the cat considerable pain because she chokes, coughs, and drools—she is very sick! The mucous membrane glows red and becomes swollen with water (edematous). When the cat opens her mouth, a foul odor exudes from her throat. Her temperature, however, is only a little over 103 degrees Fahrenheit. What to do?

Apis 3: is recommended when the mucous membrane is filled with water (edematous);

Belladonna 4: if the throat is very red; or

Mercurius solubilis 6: if the inflammation is severe and smells strongly. If the inflammation has spread to the tongue, the cat's saliva is abundant and she cannot eat or drink (she sits bent over her food dish but does not eat). In this case, administer **Baptisia 3.**

Inflammation of the Larynx (Laryngitis)

An inflammation of the larynx is the likely cause if a cat meows differently than she normally does. If she can still meow at all, the sound is raw and hoarse.

Pressure on the larynx causes pain and coughing. In addition, the cat has difficulty swallowing and she will have a fever of approximately 104 degrees Fahrenheit.

The remedy of choice is **Spongia 6.** At the beginning, it should be administered every two hours until improvement is noticeable. Thereafter, administer three times a day until the laryngitis is cured.

In young cats it is entirely possible that a foreign body (a bone, needle, etc.) might be caught in the throat.

Foreign Bodies in the Throat

Needles with thread, fish bones, and bone splinters are among the foreign bodies which can get caught in cats' throats. Such objects can cause coughing, scratching with the paw on the throat, or choking.

If you can retrieve the foreign body with a tweezers, it spares the cat the anesthetic. The veterinarian will, with or without x-rays, have to search for the foreign body.

Growths in the Larynx

Such a diagnosis is only possible under narcosis. Often, the veterinarian will find a polyp that is responsible for vague symptoms and lengthy, unsuccessful treatments.

In the past, benign growths have been treated with **Thuja**. Malignant growths, recognizable by their bad smell and verified with x-ray, are unfortunately not treatable.

Respiratory Organs

Bronchitis (Coughs) and Inflammation of the Lungs (Pneumonia)

Bronchitis refers to the inflammation of the mucous membranes of the bronchial tubes. It can be caused by the introduction of viruses or bacteria and is characterized by a cough, a fever of up to 104 degrees Fahrenheit and labored breathing.

If bronchitis spreads into the lungs, an inflammation of the lungs accompanied by a high fever (approximately 105 degrees) can develop. The labored breathing is particularly pronounced, exhalation appears very painful, and coughing fits may occur. The cat lies around lethargically and apathetically, the very picture of misery without the least appetite.

What to do? Must good advice always be expensive? Not at all! What you need is two remedies:

> **Bryonia 6** and
> **Phosphorus 12**

These two remedies should be used alternately every two hours until the danger has passed and improvement is obvious.

Adminster the remedies six times a day: 8:00 A.M., 10:00 A.M. and 12:00 P.M., as well as 4:00 P.M., 6:00 P.M., and 8:00 P.M. This holds true for bronchitis that is just starting as well as for a fully developed inflammation of the lungs.

Follow an old principle—with increasing improvement, administer the remedy less frequently. It is worthwhile.

No antibiotics, no cortisone, no antihistamines, no injections, no artificial foods should be given. You must simply devote two or three days entirely to your cat.

Other possibilities:

Drawn-out bronchitis with a constant cough and slimy discharge should be treated with **Hepar sulphuris 12** administered three times a day. If the chronic cough is part of a cold, you might consider **Sticta pulmonaria 3**.

Bronchitis with coughing fits and rasping breath such that you are afraid the cat might suffocate improves if you give the cat **Ipecacuanha 6**.

Bronchitis that becomes worse at night and is accompanied by palpitations of the heart requires **Drosera**.

Inflammation of the Pleura (Pleurisy)

The pleura cover the lungs and the inside of the chest wall.

A cat with pleurisy displays the following symptoms:

At the beginning, pleurisy is dry. A high fever and short, labored breaths indicate the pain that the dry, weak cough causes.

Later, fluid accumulates in the chest and presses the lung tissues together. The result is extreme shortness of breath.

At the beginning of the inflammation when the fluid is just starting to accumulate, homeopathy has a wonderful trick in its bag: **Bryonia.**

You should give **Bryonia 30** and, if necessary, give **Bryonia 200.** The cat's condition should improve noticeably: first her general condition, and then her appetite. If you listen to her breathing on the third day, you will be amazed at the faintness of the traces of rasping breath. A minimum of medication a-chieves a complete cure within a few days. And this holds true not only for cats, but for all animals and also for human beings.

If much fluid has already accumulated (you can determine this by listening to the cat's chest when she breathes), then her chances for recovery, even with the most attentive care, are not good with homeopathic care alone. Often, the veterinarian must vacuum the fluid out of the cat's lungs. You should definitely take her to the veterinarian and let him have a look at her, as tuberculosis might play a role here.

Otherwise, an attempt at further treatment can be made with **Arsenicum album** or **Mercurius solubilis,** but treatment should really be the domain of the experienced veterinarian, as with every type of pleurisy or dropsy of the pleura (hydro-thorax). Mention should also be made of the fact that lung cancer is not unknown in cats. If cancer appears, it cannot be effectively treated with homeopathic (or any other) methods.

3

Heart and Circulatory System

Problems with the heart and circulatory system occur rarely in cats because cats have the ability to use their strength sparingly. In contrast to the dog, the cat's movements are very economical. Thus, such circulatory problems occur only in older cats. The veterinarian must be the one to determine whether the heart muscle or cardiac valve is damaged, and treatment should be left primarily up to him.

Weakness of the Heart Muscle
(Myocardial Insufficiency)

Crataegus 1* has proven effective in cases of damage to the heart muscle. This condition is characterized by lethargy, shortness of breath, and reduced appetite. The heart pumps hard (maximal heartbeat) and the pulse. (In young animals a normal pulse reaches 140; in older animals it is usually between 100 and 120.)

Put ten globules of the remedy in each dish of food—at the beginning three times a day, then later twice a day.

Failure of the Cardiac Valve

In case of damage to or failure of the cardiac valve, administer **Convallaria 3** three times a day.

Typically, a cat with a badly damaged cardiac valve will keep her head elevated as much as possible, as her difficulties increase when she lies down.

Weakness of the Circulatory System

Acute weakness of the circulatory system can occur after extreme exertion. The cat may collapse or experience weakness of the intestines or diarrhea. Put a few drops of **Veratrum album 4** on the mucous membranes of the mouth or the front paws (she will lick them up when she cleans herself). This remedy is quick and effective.

Blood Clots (Thrombosis)

A blood clot (thrombosis) is the probable cause if the afflicted extremity is lamed and cold, loses sensation, and the pawpads are darkened by the disturbance in circulation.

Thrombosis only occurs in old age; **Lachesis 12** and **Secale cornutum 6** are recommended for treatment.

4

Digestive Organs

Stomach

In general a cat's stomach is robust and resistant and can tolerate great quantities of food.

Hairballs

It is only natural that during the cleaning of her coat, hairs enter the cat's stomach and form balls there. These balls are subsequently vomited up after she chews on grass. In order to minimize the number of hairballs in your cat's stomach, you should brush her regularly.

The vomiting up of hairballs is nothing to worry about since every cat does it from time to time. You should only be careful that your cat always has access to fresh grass; otherwise she may vomit up her food. For indoor cats, plant some grass or barley in a pot and put it in a sunny corner of the kitchen. A cat will carefully choose just the right blade of grass, for grass contains vitamins and minerals essential for her good health.

If the hairballs block the intestines, a teaspoonful of salad oil for young cats and a tablespoonful for older cats can work wonders. After six to eight hours, the blockage is gone. You can choose among olive oil, salad oil, or the oil from a sardine can. The first two should be put in the cat's food, but the cat will slurp up the sardine oil of her own accord, as cats love this tasty oil.

One weekly dosage of **Sulphur 30** while the cat is shedding shortens the period of shedding.

Mouth Odor

Tartar buildup, bad teeth, or the formation of sores in the mouth are complaints familiar to everyone. The foul odor that exudes from a problem tooth can only be cured if the veterinarian takes regulative measures. Breath that is sweetish and smells like urine indicates a problem with the kidneys—you should take a cat exhibiting this symptom to the veterinarian immediately.

Mouth odor can occur even if a cat has healthy teeth. Here, the causes lie deeper and are related to chronic disturbances in the stomach, intestines, or metabolism.

Administer **Carbo vegetalis 6** or **12** and **Nux vomica 6** or **12** three times a day for fourteen days. These remedies cleanse the digestive tract, thus removing the causes of bad breath.

A foul mouth and body odor when a cat is in heat should be treated with **Sulphur 6**.

Vomiting

Periodic vomiting, as sometimes occurs after the intake of grass or in order to remove hairballs from the stomach, is normal and not a sign of illness. By vomiting, the body rids itself of harmful substances. If a cat vomits more than once and the vomit has white foam on it, yet the cat is generally in good condition, administer a few dosages of **Ipecacuanha 6**.

Dry-heaving can be caused by an imbalance in the secretions of the stomach. Sometimes a lack of hydrochloric acid is accompanied by exhaustion and a craving for grass and houseplants. In the case of an excess of stomach acids, a cat will often vomit after she has eaten.

If you suspect an imbalance of hydrochloric acid, it is useless to determine whether there is too much or too little acid present. Of course you could run laboratory tests to find this out, but the homeopathic remedies recommended in this book regulate and can cure either a lack or an excess of stomach acids.

Administer the remedies **Pulsatilla 4** and **Nux vomica 6** every two hours until improvement is noticeable.

Vomiting can have many causes in cats. In every case, it is good to offer the cat chamomile or fennel tea for a few days instead of water, but do this only if the cat likes the tea. If she refuses the tea, change back to water.

A variation of vomiting is pylorospasm, or cramping of the aesophagus. If a single kitten in a litter vomits and cannot keep food down, the cause is most likely pylorospasmus. During the time a kitten is nursing, **Aethusa 3–30** can cure the spasms. Later in life, there are various remedies for the various illness profiles — there are different degrees of illness between a periodic cramping of the aesophagus and a frequent cramping of the valve at the end of the stomach. In any case, repeated vomiting without an obvious cause is an indication of spasms. Also noticeable are the increasing dehydration of the organism, marked especially by dry, loose skin. Various remedies should be considered for treatment, first and foremost **Nux vomica 6** or **12** and **Magnesium phosphoricum 6**, along with frequent, small meals with a lot of fluids.

Inflammation of the Mucous Membranes of the Stomach (Gastritis)

Indigestible plants consumed by the cat in place of grass, the intake of perfume or dishwater, harmful substances which enter the body when the cat cleans her fur, food that is too cold, worm infestation, or an infection can all be causes of stomach complaints in cats.

If stomach problems become more serious, look for the trio symptoms characteristic of gastritis: vomiting, loss of appetite, and stomachache.

When a cat with gastritis is lifted by her stomach, she will complain. She may sit curled up in a cool corner or lie flat in a cool place and change places when one gets too warm. Every now and then she will drink some water but will vomit it shortly thereafter.

Treatment should follow according to the cause: if you suspect a poisoning or an infection, or if the cat vomits and has a high fever, take her to the veterinarian immediately. Otherwise, the following list of homeopathic medicines may be useful.

Pulsatilla 4 and **Nux vomica 6** are the recommended remedies for stomach complaints with unclear origins. They work well in most cases—as long as poisoning and infection can be ruled out. Use in alternation.

Arsenicum album 6 is the best remedy for consumption of rancid food or meat. The feces (often diarrhea) smells like dead meat, the cat seeks warmth, and water that is consumed often and in small quantities is vomited up immediately.

Carbo vegetabilis 6 and **Nux vomica 6** are used in case of the chronic form of gastritis. Characteristic symptoms are a capricious appetite, frequent vomiting, gas buildup and rumbling in the body.

Ferrum metallicum 6 provides reliable relief in cases where the cat's appetite varies widely. Typically the cat will eat normally for two or three days, then will eat next to nothing for two or three days. Here, the probable cause is an imbalance of iron in the system. **Ferrum** will safely correct such imbalances.

Diet: first, a day of fasting! Then give the cat small portions of lean meat heated for a short time and lightly salted.

You should always have chamomile tea and water available for the cat.

Diseases of the Pancreas (Pancreatitis) and Diabetes

If the pancreas becomes diseased, the cat's prognosis is not so rosy. Acute disturbances are more unusual than chronic disturbances, which can lead to weight loss following an appetite that seems large at the beginning. Other symptoms are feces which are frequently oily-shiny, unusual thirst, and dehydration.

Treatment: **Haronga 4 + Iris 6**, a preparation which should be administered three times a day—or before each feeding.

Disorders of the pancreas are often accompanied by diabetes. Symptoms of more advanced diabetes are constant thirst and urination, eczema, cataracts, weight loss, and lethargy.

In most cases, the insulin-producing organ is so badly damaged that homeopathic remedies for diabetes such as, **Phosphoric acid, Kreosotum**, or **Syzygium** are seldom successful, though this medicines should be tried individually for at least one month each.

The pancreas, the organ targeted for treatment, is not in any condition to react in such a way that it could re-regulate and cure the imbalances in the insulin system.

There remains only the possibility of injecting insulin every day—but what cat will tolerate daily injections? And what cat-owner can stand such a treatment?

Diet: Feed the cat a little lean meat (primarily chicken or lamb), eggs, and low-fat milk.

It is interesting to note that a latent potential for diabetes can be activated by high dosages of cortisone.

Intestines

Inflammation of the Intestines (Enteritis/Diarrhea)

An inflammation of the mucous membranes of the intestine—often accompanied by an inflammation of the mucous membranes of the stomach—makes its presence known if the cat has extreme diarrhea. Such an inflammation can be caused by a virus or bacteria, defects in food, or worms, and coccidiosia or poisoning can also play a role.

Consistency, color and smell of the feces determine the correct choice of a homeopathic remedy. Inflammations that crop up suddenly and are accompanied by a drop-off in the cat's strength require treatment with antibiotics by the veterinarian. Less severe inflammations can be treated with the following remedies:

Pulsatilla 6: Pulsatilla diarrhea always contains mucus and each stool looks different: sometimes green, sometimes yellow, sometimes watery, sometimes firmer, but always slimy. In spite of the loss of liquids due to the diarrhea, the cat drinks surprisingly little. The cause is often food that is too cold or too fatty.

Arsenicum album 6: Diarrhea at night indicates the need for **Arsenicum album.** The stool smells like dead meat and is produced often, but only in small quantities. It can contain blood and mucus and causes the cat a lot of discomfort. Because the cat is anxious and restless, she changes her place often and expresses a desire for warmth. The cat drinks often, but only a little each time.

Arsenicum 6, administered every two hours, can help quickly and safely. If no effect is noticeable, however, it should not be continued for more than two days. **Arsenicum** diarrhea is caused by defects in food of animal origin prepared under improper hygienic conditions or moldy food that should have been heated before feeding. Rapid exhaustion, weight loss, and restlessness are typical for **Arsenicum.**

Mercurius solubilis 6: This remedy becomes necessary if the cat develops a noticeable urge to evacuate her bowels. She hardly climbs out of her litter box since she has the feeling that something else must come out. The stool is greenish-yellow and possibly also bloody. The cat is very irritable.

Podophyllum 4: Of use in cases of so-called "hydrant-stool," where the yellowish, watery diarrhea flows as if from a water faucet.

Leptandra 3: Effective when the diarrhea smells like tea, the intestines rumble a lot, and defecation is very watery. Frequently, the cause is unrecognized damage to the liver. Attempts at treatment with other remedies have failed.

Aloe socotrina 6: This remedy is called for when the cat loses bowel control. Defecation occurs entirely without pressure; the stool simply falls out. It is yellow, thin and slimy, and accompanied by flatulence and discomfort—especially in the early morning and during urination.

With these remedies, you have a handle on the general treatment of diarrhea. Two additional illness profiles are for **Phosphorus 12** (whitish or whitish-gray stool with no sign of weakness in the body) and **Dulcamara 4** (diarrhea apparently caused by dampness).

Naturally the veterinarian must reach for antibiotics in cases of extreme inflammations of the intestines. If you are observant and careful in your choice of remedy, however, homeopathy can be of help. Homeopathy is not a matter of faith, but rather a cure based on observation, which in most cases brings healing without antibiotics.

Diet for cases of diarrhea: No milk, no fat, no oil, but rather chamomile, fennel, or black tea, cooked liver, and hard-boiled eggs.

Note: The anus of a healthy animal is always clean and not soiled like that of a sick animal.

Constipation

Cats that lead a normal life seldom suffer from constipation. They have enough activity and eat what they find and what they need. But how many of them must live in the city without the opportunity to venture outside!

Defecation can become problematic for some indoor cats. Sometimes a cat will only defecate every third, fourth, eighth, or even every tenth day. Old cats suffer the most from constipation.

You should take care to see that your cat defecates regularly, for once the large intestine becomes stopped up with feces, it will seldom return to its original size.

Constipation is not necessarily an indication of serious illness if it occurs only every now and then. Raw liver, milk, cream, or sardine oil can relieve constipation. If these remedies do not work, pour a tablespoonful of olive oil into a spoon heated in hot water (on which only a few drops remain) and add to food. Brush the cat firmly and play with her a lot; this will encourage defecation.

Pressure on the urethra can cause urine to back up into the kidneys; vomiting, paralysis of the hindquarters, and even death can result.

If the stool is not evacuated every day or every second day, you should employ the proven remedies listed below:

In acute cases, administer one dosage every two hours until improvement is noticeable. In less serious situations, administer one dosage two to three times a day. These remedies should restore the normal functioning of the intestines and are therefore not "laxatives."

Heavy, slow cats that like to eat a lot, are "overweight" because of a lack of exercise, and can defecate only after consuming milk or cream can be cured with **Calcarea carbonica 12**. This remedy regulates defecation and solves other problems as well since it corrects any imbalance of calcium.

Another type of cat is just as slow, phlegmatic, heavy, and sad. In addition, she is anxious and jumpy. The fur is dry, raw, and brittle. You can see eczema with a secretion that looks and feels like honey. Disturbances in the growth of the claws, scars, the accumulation of crusts on the skin or stinking sweat on the paw-pads may be present—but not necessarily all at the same time. The recommended remedy is **Graphites**.

Cats that run frequently to the litter box, strain futilely and only manage to produce a little hard feces after a long attempt at defecation need **Nux vomica**.

Then there are cats whose constipation is tortuous and who manage to defecate only with the greatest of effort. When they have finally succeeded in defecating, the feces appears far too large for such a small animal. Not only this, but the feces is also hard and dry. The cure for this malady is **Bryonia**.

The patient should receive these remedies until improvement is noticeable, which can take up to fourteen days. If the digestive process is re-regulated and seems to be harmonious once again, the remedies are no longer necessary. If a relapse should occur, administer one dosage a day for a few days in the cat's food.

Protracted constipation can lead to vomiting, loss of appetite, and apathy. If the hardened lumps of feces can be felt through the stomach tissues, you must administer injections of physiological salts: one tablespoonful salt to one liter of warm water.

Foreign Bodies in the Intestines

A foreign body in the intestines is not the domain of homeopathic remedies, but rather of surgical intervention. If a complete blockage of the intestines occurs—as can happen in younger animals who sometimes swallow toys—and the cat vomits and cannot defecate, then take her to the veterinarian immediately!

Prolapse of the Anus

All such occurrences, whether they concern the anus or the vagina, require the assistance of the veterinarian. After veterinary treatment, **Arnica 6** in alternation with **Hypericum 3** administered four times a day can be of good service.

Intestinal Parasites

In mild cases, signs of illness are often not even perceptible. Symptoms to watch for are lackluster fur, diarrhea, constipation, weight loss, and/or vomiting.

Roundworms are often found in young cats. Older cats are immune and are more susceptible to tapeworms. The roundworms are four to six centimeters long and live in the small intestine. Their larvae wander through the liver and lungs where they can cause rasping and coughing and may reproduce. Some of the larvae may conceal themselves in the body and only reactivate if the animal becomes pregnant. This can be a cause of worm infestation in young cats even if the mother cat appears quite healthy.

A distended stomach and anemia indicate an infestation of roundworm. The cat may also vomit up worms. In extreme cases, the cat will lose weight, be very nervous, drool, be thirstier than normal, and have diarrhea.

Hookworms take hold in the small intestine, "hooking" themselves into the wall of the intestine and sucking up blood. The cat will gradually become weak and anemic. Blood may appear in the stool or the cat may have bloody diarrhea every now and then.

Tapeworms are present in the feces or in the hairs around the cat's anus. Tapeworms can be recognized by their flat, noodle-like appendages which at first move, then later dry up like little rice-kernels.

Weight loss, frequent diarrhea, and scratching and licking at the anus may indicate an infestation of these parasites. They are carried to the cat by fleas, which when swallowed successfully infect the cat with tapeworms.

Infection can also occur through contact with mice or rats.

A diagnosis of Coccidiosis is only possible when stool samples are examined under a microscope. Diarrhea is mixed with blood.

There are various ways of combating parasitic infestations:

1. You can administer a worm medicine prescribed by your veterinarian. Today, these remedies are very mild and reliable and are effective in cases of worm infestation and the problematic Echinococcus.

2. If you prefer not to use or believe that your cat is too weak for such a cure, then you can use homeopathic remedies to achieve the same effect. The worms will not be killed off— homeopathy always has respect for life and thus never kills. Rather the "terrain" of the intestinal tract will be strengthened so that the worms are excreted. Naturally this takes some time. The following remedies are recommended:

Roundworm: Abrotanum 3 for seven days
Tapeworms: Cina 4 for seven days
Hookworms: Carduus marianus 4 for ten days
Coccidiosia: Phosphoric acid 6 for seven days

Administer these remedies three times a day, then administer **Calcarea carbonica 200** once as a conclusion.

You can also attempt to rid the intestine of worms by changing the cat's diet. The best diet for this purpose is light fare with little meat.

Liver

The liver is often described as a chemical factory. Its tasks are many and varied, and therefore damage to the liver can have serious consequences.

Along with the kidneys, the liver is one of the most important waste-removal organs in the body. The liver has the ability to regenerate itself and can function adequately until a large part of the organ is sick or destroyed. The full regeneration of the liver can take quite a long time, depending on the nature of the injury.

If a cat comes into contact with poisonous substances such as motor oil or pesticides while cleaning her fur, an acute stomach or liver ailment can result.

Other causes for injury to the liver are the accumulation of poisonous substances in the cat's system due to overfeeding, viruses, bacteria, worm infestation, and heart and kidney ailments.

Diseases of the Liver

The diagnosis "damage to the liver" is not easy to confirm and can only be made by the veterinarian. The vague symptoms of liver damage are digestive disturbances accompanied by vomiting, varying appetite, greasy stool, urine that is often the color of clay or dark yellow, and a perceptible lethargy and apathy.

An excellent remedy that has proven useful for treatment of the liver is the South American stone-blossom **Flor de Piedra 4**. This herb is not an official homeopathic medicine in the U.S., but is sometimes available in herb stores. This remedy should be administered regularly for a period of time.

> In the first week, 1 tablet three times a day;
> in the second week, 1 tablet twice a day;
> and afterwards, one dosage a day.

This remedy works specifically on the liver. An apparent downturn in the patient's condition on the third or fourth day is possible and should be viewed as a sign of healing, but need not always occur.

During the course of treatment, it is a good idea to put some dextrose in the cat's drinking water (1 tablespoonful in ¼ liter water). If this causes the cat to have diarrhea, however, the dosage must be reduced or eliminated entirely. This cure is valuable in acute and chronic cases of damage to the liver.

Chronic liver damage is a chapter unto itself. It is often hopeless because of the progressive hardening of the liver and the subsequent dropsy of the peritoneum (ascites).

Whomever wishes to attempt treatment should administer

> one dosage of **Nux vomica 30** on the first day,
> one dosage of **Phosphorus 30** on the second day,
> one dosage of **Lycopodium 30** on the third day

and so on, until—possibly—improvement becomes obvious in the general condition of the patient. If this happens, try not giving the cat these remedies to see whether the improvement lasts.

In the case of the type of cirrhosis of the liver that progresses with the extreme enlargement of the liver, **Carduus marianus 30** is recommended. Administer one dosage three times a day. Good results have been obtained with this remedy at least twice in the last thirty years, but it cannot be considered a reliable cure by any means.

Jaundice

Jaundice occurs in cats every now and then. It is easily recognizable since it colors all of the mucous membranes yellow—those of the eye, the oral cavity, the anus, and the vagina. Discoloration may also be apparent in the portions of the skin that are not so thickly covered with hair.

There are various causes, and without going into them

in detail, they are all marked by a deterioration in the general condition, great thirst, reduced appetite, frequent vomiting, and a coating on the tongue.

A cat exhibiting these symptoms needs one dosage of **Natrum sulfuricum** every two hours and, with improvement, four times a day. Improvement should set in relatively quickly. In addition, administer **Chelidonium 30** once a day.

Weight Loss and Weight Gain

Weight loss in the best years of a cat's life can have many causes. Therefore, the veterinarian should examine the cat thoroughly and attempt to diagnose the problem. This is often easier said than done.

If the veterinarian can find nothing wrong with the cat, administer three to five drops of **Condurango 3** three times a day for two weeks.

A healthy male cat should weigh between three and five kilograms (5 to 11 pounds). A healthy female cat should weigh no more than two and a half to four kilograms. It is possible that exceptions may be necessary for unusually large animals, but it is certainly true that overweight cats have a shorter life span and are sick more often than other cats.

If a cat is supposed to lose weight, it is a good idea to present her every now and then with something she has never eaten before. She is always subject to the whims of her appetite and is not likely to dig into unfamiliar food immediately. If nothing else is offered to her, a meal is thus skipped. This is not unhealthy, but to the contrary, it helps the cat lose weight and stay healthy.

Once in my practice, I had a large, fat tomcat that showed no appetite. I could find absolutely nothing wrong with him, and since he appeared to be feeling good, I decided it would be best if his owner simply waited to see what would happen.

The game lasted more than twenty-four days before the tomcat started to eat again. He lived happily for many years after that. This really happens! There are documented cases of fasts by cats that have lasted as long as six weeks.

The Feeding of Sick Cats

Sick cats should be fed what they like to eat. If a cat loves fresh eggs, a few drops of red wine mixed in can work wonders and stimulate the appetite. Give the cat her usual food: raw meat, fish, prepared cat food, or whatever she is used to and can readily digest.

You can feed the cat small ground-meat meatballs by pushing them in through the corners of her mouth. This may become necessary if she suffers from the form of feline distemper in the course of which sores form on the edge of the tongue that make the intake of food impossible.

It is a good idea to put dextrose in the water of a sick cat (as long as this does not give her diarrhea), as this also stimulates the appetite. Stir one teaspoonful of dextrose into one cup of water.

Milk is not an appropriate food for sick cats. It should be given sparingly even to healthy cats since too much milk can lead to stomach and intestinal disorders and diarrhea.

5

Ligaments, Tendons, Joints, and Bones

Ligaments, Tendons, and Joints

Sprains (Distorsion)

A temporary dislocation of a joint, a tear in a ligament and a partial tearing of a ligament are all referred to as sprains. Sprains sometimes occur after a cat jumps down from a great height.

Symptoms of a sprain are sudden lameness accompanied by a swelling of the joint. The normal structure of the bones is not affected.

In case of sprains, **Arnica 6** or **30** (bruising of the skin or soft tissue as a result of trauma) and **Rhus toxicodendron 30** (tearing of a ligament) have proven effective if administered four times a day in alternation.

The combination of **Arnica 3, Ruta 3, and Hypericum 3** administered in equal parts three to four times a day also has healing qualities.

Dislocation (Luxation)

Luckily, lasting dislocations of the lower jaw, elbow, or hip seldom occur in cats. The dislocation of a joint can be accompanied by the tearing of muscle tissue, tendons, or blood vessels, or the breaking-off of bone splinters.

In the case of a partial dislocation of a joint, the entire joint is not affected.

For the cat, however, this is already bad enough. You will be able to see that the shape and angle of the joint are different than normal, and the cat may be severely lamed. She may also avoid standing on the affected limb and suffer much pain. The best thing you can do is take the cat to the veterinarian so he can reposition the dislocated limb while the cat is anesthetized. Repositioning must be done quickly if it is to be successful and proceed without complications. Afterwards, quiet rest is the best remedy.

Arnica 30 administered every four hours is recommended for dislocations because it takes away the pain and encourages quick healing. It should be continued for at least three days.

Inflammation of the Joints (Arthritis)

Excessive force is the most common cause of an acute inflammation of a joint. Other possible causes are sprains and dislocations. Often, however, the cause is unclear. Depending on which joint is affected, the cat can be lamed in the hip, in the knee, or in the shoulder. Noteworthy is the fact that the cat experiences pain even when the joint is moved for her, i.e., if a person moves the swollen, feverish joint. X-rays do not reveal much about an arthritic joint.

In case of chronic arthritis that no longer hurts, you can sometimes feel a crunching or grinding in the joint if you move the cat's limb.

The best therapy is quiet rest. If the cat runs around too much, lock her in a transport cage.

For acute arthritis, administer **Bryonia 6** and **Rhus toxicodendron 12** every two hours in alternation. This should bring quick relief and then healing.

For chronic arthritis, administer one dosage of **Bryonia 30** mornings and one dosage of **Rhus toxicodendron 30** evenings over a longer period of time.

Bones

Broken Bones (Fractures)

The prognosis for healing the broken bones of a cat is good. However, you must take the cat to the veterinarian immediately so he can determine which bones are affected and reposition them correctly while she is anesthetized.

In the case of a fracture of the upper part of the leg, an operation may be necessary. Most other fractures can be treated adequately with bandages reinforced with plaster or splints. If in the case of a fracture of the upper part of the leg you do not wish to allow the veterinarian to put a pin in the leg, you can wait and allow nature to heal the fracture.

It is important that the cat be placed in a transport basket or cage so her movement is restricted. The floor of the container must be flat and should not be heavily padded. In order to relieve her pain, the cat lies down on her injured side, and if the affected area comes in contact with the flat floor of the container, this can have a healing effect. The healing of a fracture generally takes two to three weeks. Even if the cat is still a little lame at the beginning, everything will regulate itself in the course of time.

The homeopathic remedies most likely to promote the development of callouses (which serve to fuse the ends of the bones) are **Calcarea phosphorica 4** and **Symphytum 2** or **6** administered four times a day each in alternation.

These remedies can also help in situations where, for unexplained reasons, callous development does not occur as it should in cases of spontaneous fractures (so-called Pseudoarthrosis).

The most common cause of broken bones is traffic accidents. Occasionally a cat will break a bone falling from a great height, but sprains and the discharge of blood are the usual consequences of a fall.

Even when a cat falls from five stories up, she is more likely to suffer sprains and a slight concussion than broken bones. The reason for this is that during a fall, cats have the ability to regulate the position of their bodies so that the stress of landing will be equally borne by all four extremities. The cat literally falls on her feet.

Arnica 6 is useful for treating the shock of an accident. It will also encourage the reabsorption of blood from around a broken bone or anywhere else. The swelling that occurs around a fresh fracture permits only the application of a temporary dressing of cotton and bandages. A permanent dressing (with or without metal splints) may be put on later after the swelling has subsided. **Arnica** should be administered once an hour on the day of the accident and four times a day on the following days. Once the permanent dressing is in place, stop giving the cat Arnica and instead give her **Calcarea phosphorica 4** and **Symphytum 2** or **6** in alternation, as these remedies will encourage the "knitting together" of the broken bones.

Fracture of the Pelvis

A fractured pelvis is usually the result of a traffic accident. A cat with a fractured pelvis cannot lift herself on her hindquarters and will appear lamed. X-rays can confirm the diagnosis if you cannot feel the fracture with your hands or hear the so-called crepitations, the rubbing-together of the ends of the bones. Fractures of the pelvis can be simple or compound.

Possible complications are the discharge of blood (which needs time to be reabsorbed) or the tearing of large blood vessels, which can, in extreme cases, lead to death.

The cat needs peace and quiet, a sensible diet, and the proper remedies. Diet is important because the pelvis, in the process of being broken and healing, can contract. If this occurs, constipation must be avoided at all costs. Therefore, feed the cat light food and mix one tablespoonful of paraffin into her food every day or two.

The recommended remedy is three dosages of **Calcarea phosphorica 4** and two dosages of **Symphytum 2** or **6** daily. As this quickly becomes a tiresome routine for the cat-owner, it should be noted that another possibility is for the veterinarian to inject these remedies in the potency **30** two times a week. Yet another way of administering these remedies is to crush them and mix with the cat's food twice a day and cover the cat's front paws with them three times a day since she will consume the remedies when she cleans herself.

Finally, it does not happen often that a cat-owner must care for his cat so intensively, but broken bones are a serious event in her life that may require time and patience to heal.

A hairline fracture, a crack in the bone that is only perceptible with the help of x-rays, can also be treated with **Calcarea phosphorica 4** and **Symphytum 2** or **6**. These remedies should be administered four times a day each in alternation for several days.

Disturbances in Bone Formation (Softness of the Bones)

This evil disease, called various names by veterinarians, afflicts young cats between three and six months of age. Siamese cats are especially prone to this disease. The cat shuns movement, she has difficulty walking, she limps, and in the worst case, her legs are crippled.

The cause can be an imbalance in the diet—for example, if the kitten eats only meat and lacks carbohydrates and dry food. A change of diet is critical: feed the kitten a only a little meat and supplement her diet with fish, dry food, and dairy products.

Another possible cause is that the kitten lacks calcium—and cartilage. Despite the presence of sufficient calcium in her diet, the cat's body is not able to store the calcium where it is most needed, namely in the bones. This condition can be cured with homeopathically prepared **Calcarea.**

On the first day, administer **Calcarea carbonica 6** three times. On the second day, administer **Calcarea phosphorica 6** three times, and so on, alternating each day for two weeks.

Once a week give the cat a dosage of **Silicea 200** until she appears just as fresh and full of life as other cats her age.

Because some researchers assert that this disturbance in bone formation is inherited, do not attempt to breed cats with this condition.

Paralysis

Paralysis after an accident can be treated with **Arnica 6.**

Arnica should be administered as follows:

- once every hour on the first day
- once every two hours on the second day
- three times a day from the third day on for as long as necessary

A temporary "paralysis" of the hindquarters can occur in cases of extreme constipation, where the constipation must naturally be regarded as the cause.

Extremely rare is radial paralysis. Such cases of paralysis can occur if the cat's front paws get stuck somewhere and the nerve is pinched. A cat with this condition has trouble moving her front paws and drags herself slowly along.

Successful treatment of radial paralysis can be achieved with **Hypericum 3**. Administer five dosages on the first day and three dosages a day from the second day on until the paralysis is cured.

Even in early youth, a cat that is fed only meat and no carbohydrates or dry food can suffer from paralysis. A poor diet can cause improper development of the bone structure and can even lead to broken bones, mostly during the time the cat is teething (from the fourth to the sixth month).

6

Reproductive Organs

Castration of the Male Cat, Sterilization of the Female Cat

The keeping of cats in big cities is difficult unless they are castrated, as otherwise they will mark their entire house or apartment with their scent when they reach sexual maturity at about seven months. There are, of course, exceptions, but more often than not such odors become a problem for cat-owners.

When a cat is neutered, several common problems are avoided: the cat will not reproduce uncontrolled, fights among tomcats will not occur as frequently, and abandoned cats will not overrun our cities.

Neutered animals are tamer than animals that have not been neutered, and they maintain their figure and temperament better if the operation is successful and performed after the gonads are fully developed. Sterilized females are particularly likely to let the dependent and harmonious aspects of their character shine through.

In the case of a sterilization undertaken too early, fat deposits develop late; a paunch may appear around the teats.

The operation must be performed by a veterinarian while the cat is under general anesthesia. This happens only once in a cat's life, and it must, even in the case of a tomcat, be done while the cat can feel no pain.

Follow-up treatments are not necessary. One tablet of **Arnica 30** administered three times a day for three days after the operation stimulates rapid healing without complications.

The removal of the gonads does not make the cat completely gender-neutral. The sexual drive is only dampened somewhat. Female cats can still act as if they are in heat and may sometimes be serenaded by tomcats—but naturally much more discreetly and softly.

There is no homeopathic remedy that can completely and permanently suppress the cat's natural drives. Homeopathy is always "sympathetic," never opposed to life, and so there is no homeopathic remedy that can harm life or assist in the killing of a living being.

Midwifery

Luckily, cats know well how to have kittens and only rarely need help. From puberty on, cats are capable of multiple pregnancies and make excellent mothers.

Release of the egg occurs between forty and sixty hours after intercourse. During pregnancy, when the cat's hormones are extremely active, she may be more vigilant than usual, eat more than she normally does, and search for the food that tastes the best to her (including particular kinds of grass). She is caring for herself and preparing for the birth of her kittens, which usually occurs after sixty or sixty-one days of pregnancy (depending on the breed of cat, pregnancy can last between fifty-six and sixty-five days).

The question of whether or not a cat is pregnant can only

be answered after four weeks, when her midsection and her teats become enlarged and turn pink.

Additional vitamins or dietary supplements are unnecessary for cats that eat a proper diet. A preventative worm cure in the first third of the pregnancy is recommended.

Prior to the birth of the kittens, you should set up a whelping-basket for the cat. This basket (or carton) should not be too large, because cats like to retreat to a quiet, protected and somewhat dark place before they give birth. A mother cat feels particularly comfortable in a covered bed (you can cover a carton with a length of cloth). You should put some newspaper, as mother cats like to shred newspaper on the bottom to make a nest for themselves and their kittens. It is exciting and educational for children to be able to observe the birth of kittens.

Shortly before giving birth, the cat will become restless since she senses that something new and unknown to her is about to happen. At first, the labor pains seem to resemble pressure on the bladder.

What does she do then? She runs once or twice to the litter box, but has no success there. Some feline mothers-to-be look with surprise at the empty litter box and wonder what is happening to them.

But finally, the cat will turn to the whelping-basket. At this point, the first phase of birth begins: the amniotic fluid moistens the birth-passages and the cat licks it up. Soon, labor pains begin and the first kitten will appear—it does not matter whether it comes into the world head or tail first. Either way, it does not cause problems for its mother. The coating on the kitten is licked off along with any remaining amniotic fluid; the mother cat awakens her kitten into the world with a few firm strokes of her tongue. The afterbirth (placenta) should follow and will be eaten by the mother along with the umbilical cord. This causes milk to enter the teats. The other kittens will follow every fifteen to thirty minutes. Pauses of as long as two hours between newborns are not unusual, and kittens born later will be cared for just like the first. When the whole litter (usually four to six kittens) has been brought into the world, the mother will clean them thoroughly and nurse them.

If, four hours after the amniotic fluid has appeared, a kitten has yet to be born, then the mother needs help. This occurs very rarely.

In the case of visible labor pains, you must help the cat keep the birth passage moist. Most of the time, however, the problem is that the kitten is so large it cannot fit through the birth passage. If this is true, a Caesarian section is required. You should contact the veterinarian immediately.

If the mother cat becomes weak during labor, administer a few doses of **Secale cornutum 6** and **Caulophyllum 6**—do this every fifteen minutes, alternating between the two remedies.

It is interesting for the observer to note that the mother cat does not experience even the slightest inclination to kill or maim during the time she is giving birth. Only in light of this observation is it possible to explain how other animals (such as mice or squirrels) that she would normally kill on sight are even allowed to drink her milk—a favorite topic of illustrated magazines.

In the kittens' first weeks, you should help them defecate by massaging their rear ends, if the mother isn't doing this herself. Afterwards, remove the excrement from the whelping-basket. In the third or fourth week, the mother should teach her kittens to use the litter box. In the fourth week, the mother's previously undivided attention to her kittens will abate somewhat; they should already be fed baby food, milk, and oatmeal in addition to the nutrients they get from their mother's milk.

It is also interesting to see how cats transport their kittens.

Sometime during the time the kittens are nursing, the mother will seek out a new nest for her brood. She will then take each kitten in her mouth by the scruff of its neck and carry it to the new nest. The kitten will relax and remain quiet until its mother puts it down again. People can make use of this grip when they wish to pick adult cats up or remove them from cages: grasp the cat on the back of the neck with one hand—this is helpful and it reminds the cat of its mother.

Soon after birth, the mother cat begins weaning her kittens and teaching them what they need to know. Once a new hormonal cycle begins, the mother cat prepares herself for a renewed period of heat and a new family. After this happens, she shows little interest in her present family. The kittens should arrive in their new homes when they are between eight and ten weeks of age.

If a mother cat somehow loses her litter, you should give her something to mother; try a doll or a toy. Soon, a new period of heat should set in and she will be able to mate once again.

But if every cat-owner did things like this, what would happen? Plenty of calculations have already been made: assuming that a cat will give birth twice a year and that 2.8 kittens out of each litter survive, then after ten years there would be more than eighty million cats—calculate for yourself!

This is the reason that cats should be sterilized at the latest after the first litter of kittens, if not before.

The determination of the sex of a kitten is not as easy as it is for puppies, but it is also not as difficult as it is often reported to be. To be sure of the kitten's sex, look at both its anus and urethra. In female cats, the anus and the urethra are close to one another. In male cats, they are farther apart. If you compare two different kittens, it will quickly become clear which is which.

If the mother cat does not have enough milk for her kittens despite a good diet, **Urtica urens 30** can help her.

In pet stores, you may find preparations that stimulate milk production. These should be used only if the mother's milk dries up altogether, as they must be administered five or six times.

The mother cat should be well cared for during the time the kittens are nursing: she should be given raw chopped meat with eggs, a vitamin preparation (but not too much of this) and, naturally, also dry food.

Milk substitutes, available in many pet stores, should be used only in case of emergency—for example if the mother's milk is completely lacking. These preparations, which are available by prescription, must be fed to the kittens every three hours. Use a disposable syringe (5 ml) or a pipette to feed the kittens, making sure the kittens can suck the milk in and swallow it—they must be fed drop by drop! One meal = one teaspoonful = 5 ml from a syringe. But this quickly becomes a burden for the cat-owner.

Maybe the veterinarian can supply a nursemaid; this could also be a dog in whose litter the kittens nurse. There, the kittens will find nest-warmth and proper nutrition, which is ultimately better for them than any painstaking care you can provide.

Inflammation of the Vagina (Vaginitis)

If a cat licks her anus a lot due to a bladder infection or after a pregnancy, the vagina can become inflamed. Discharge from an inflamed vagina can be bloody-watery or pus-like. Sometimes young animals experiencing their first heat cycle suffer from this problem. They will constantly try to rub the vagina in order to make the inflammation subside.

In acute cases, **Cantharis 6** can help; in chronic cases use **Hydrastis 6** and **Kali bichromicum 6** in alternation.

Inflammation of the Uterus (Metritis)

This type of inflammation is most often due to a failure to discharge the afterbirth from the body. The afterbirth decomposes and results in a stinking, pus-like discharge accompanied by a rapid pulse, fever, and excessively moist conjunctiva. This life-threatening condition requires the attention of a veterinarian. Most veterinarians choose to treat such inflammations with antibiotics because it is critical for the kittens that the mother cat be cured as quickly as possible. A homeopathically inclined veterinarian can, according to the condition of the cat, achieve the same effect with a preparation of **Lachesis, Pyrogenium** and **Echinacea.**

A chronic inflammation of the uterus does not proceed as dramatically. Obvious is the poor general condition of the cat, her capricious appetite, weight loss and the often-interrupted discharge of blood and pus. In such circumstances, the following remedy has proven effective: **Sepia 6, Helonias 6,** and **Hydrastis 6,** in equal parts in powdered form administered three times a day until the condition is cured (this typically takes seven to fourteen days).

Festering of the Uterus (Pyometra)

This condition refers to a buildup of pus in the uterus, which causes the uterus to enlarge. Thirst and lethargy increase simultaneously.

An immediate operation to remove the afflicted uterus and ovaries is necessary. If this is not possible or not desired, you can attempt treatment with the following homeopathic remedies:

If discharge is lacking, the septic pus or buildup of water remains in the body and causes an obvious distension of the stomach. Then you should try opening the mouth of the uterus with one dosage every hour of **Pulsatilla 6** from morning until night. If, within forty-eight hours, no stream of discharge appears, an operation must be performed.

If discharge appears, however, a greenish-yellow discharge calls for **Pulsatilla 6** three times a day. A brownish discharge requires **Sepia**, and if fever accompanies this illness, you should add a few drops of **Lachesis 12** to each dosage.

A pharmaceutical preparation recommended by French homeopaths has proven effective in cases of acute and chronic inflammations of the uterus: Mix **Sepia 6**, **Helonias 6**, and **Hydrastis 6** in equal parts.

This remedy should be administered three times a day until the discharge is bloody, a sign that the mucous membranes have renewed themselves. Continue to administer it twice a day for a few days, then once a day for a time until everything is back in order. No more discharge should flow and the cat should appear happy and healthy.

Inflammation of the Teats (Mastitis)

If the mother cat somehow loses her nursing kittens, milk backs up in her teats. This can lead to an inflammation of the lacteal gland. Infection from outside the cat's body can also cause this condition, for example, if the nursing kittens leave small bite-marks on their mother's teats.

All signs of inflammation such as redness, swelling, pain, heat, and restlessness are present. Sometimes abscesses will form and sores will discharge bloody pus. Of course, the cat's general condition is not helped by the fever, the loss of appetite, and her general discomfort.

The inflammation of the teats can be cured with a series of dosages of **Belladonna 6**, administered every hour or two.

If, however, the tissue appears to be swollen with water, reddish, extremely sensitive and warm to the touch, administer **Apis 3** or **6**. Later, give the cat doses of **Lachesis 12** or **30** every two to three hours until improvement is noticeable and the cat returns to her normal condition.

Individual teats can become inflamed even if the cat is not nursing. They should be cared for in the same way.

Swellings (Tumors)

Unfortunately, tumors on the teats occur in cats, especially in old cats. Such tumors can be benign or malignant.

Benign tumors grow slowly and are clearly separated from the area surrounding them. They can occur after heat or giving birth, and at the beginning of their development, they may be brought under control with three dosages of **Phytolacca 6** daily for a lengthy period of time. **Conium 12** should also be administered if the tumors do not shrink noticeably within eight days.

Malignant tumors are a different story altogether. They grow quickly and unchecked, and they present a danger to other organs by way of the blood and lymphatic fluids. Even after an operation, they return quickly. If a histological examination reveals a carcinoma in the tissue, you can attempt to check its spread with **Conium 6** and **Calcarea fluorica 12**. The pharmacist can provide you with these remedies in small pellets which should be mixed into the cat's food at least twice a day for at least several months.

In case of weight loss accompanied by restlessness at night, also administer **Arsenicum album 6**, which should bring improvement in the cat's general condition and alleviate her pain.

In Heat

Normal heat makes its presence known through restlessness, rolling on the ground, unusual devotion, a rolling purr, and an erect tail. In indoor cats, the urge to venture outside cannot be overlooked. And how long does this last? Two or three days and possibly more.

Female indoor cats that have not been sterilized can go into heat every month (the peak periods are spring and fall). If this is the case, however, it is likely that cysts on the ovaries (due to a hormonal imbalance) are the cause. A healthy female cat should go into heat no more than three or four times a year. Too often, the neighbors hear about the cat's heat when she yowls for a tomcat; female Siamese cats are particularly likely to call loudly for a mate.

This should be cause enough for the cat-owner to take his cat to the veterinarian and have her sterilized. Furthermore, unsterilized cats are prone to be irritable and moody because they are in heat all too often. The best time for an operation is midway between two heat cycles. In cats to be used for breeding, this problem must be approached differently: here, you can try giving the cat a daily dosage of **Murex 30** until she becomes quiet once again (this can take as long as ten days). If the symptoms return, repeat the treatment. Provided the ovaries are not changed too drastically, the heat cycle should be brought under control.

7

Urinary Tract

The urinary tract includes both kidneys and their respective catheters, the bladder, and also the urethra, which in the female cat is short, and in the male cat is relatively long and constricted. The urethra is often a source of difficulties for the male cat.

Inflammation of the Bladder (Cystitis)

An inflammation of a cat's bladder can come about because she gets soaking wet or catches cold, or because of an infection. A bladder inflammation progresses in such a way that a cat-owner cannot help but notice it; the cat runs stiffly to her litter box and urinates with a bent back. Obviously this burns, for the cat looks backwards as she urinates. And she can only force out a few drops that may be bloody.

The cat's general condition does not suffer noticeably, but this complaint must be treated quickly because it too easily becomes chronic, and it can also adversely affect the kidneys.

An inflammation of the bladder in the first phase should be treated with **Belladonna 6** even if blood is mixed with the urine. Administer one dose every two hours until improvement is obvious, then three times a day for a few more days.

Another remedy is **Apis 3** or **6**, which should also be administered every two hours if the urine comes out often but in small quantities and the cat does not drink much. Warmth makes this condition worse, cold makes it better. The cat will choose to lie in a cool place. There may be some blood present in the urine. If the urine consists only of blood, however, it is high time for a treatment with **Cantharis 4** or **6** every hour or two. As a follow-up after the inflammation has subsided somewhat, give the cat **Berberis 3** or **Sulphur 6** for a few days, since these will eliminate the remains of the inflammation in the body.

Urinary Calculus

In castrated tomcats and Persian cats, the urethra can become blocked by the solid component of the urine, urinary calculus.

At first the cat is anxious and restless, she beats with her tail, meows a lot, and will not lie down. It hurts if you touch her stomach, and her posture is peculiarly arched upwards because the overfilled bladder is causing her pain. It speaks for the elasticity of the bladder that a rupture hardly ever occurs. If this condition continues for any length of time, however, urinary poisoning accompanied by vomiting and a lowered body temperature can result.

What to do?

A concerned cat-owner should try to obtain **Sabal serrulatum 3** and place one crushed tablet on the cat's gums or under her tongue every hour until she can urinate once again. If **Sabal** helps—this depends on the size of the clumps of calculus which we cannot see—then after an hour after this urination, everything should be in working order. This is one possibility for treating this condition. A second possibility is a single dosage of **Lycopodium 30** followed by hourly dosages of **Berberis 3**. These two alternatives are useful and successful if the problem is an easily dissolved lump of urinary sediments. And in general, this is the case. If the cat's condition is already more advanced, however, the only option is intervention by the veterinarian while she is under anesthesia. With time, the danger of the urine entering the bloodstream increases, and the cat can slip into a deathly coma.

Repeated difficulties indicate a significant accumulation of urinary calculus. In this case, you should attempt to treat the problem with one tablet of **Magnesium carbonica 30** and one of **Lycopodium 30** in daily alternation. This is often effective and has cured many cats in the past. The cure lasts four weeks and can be repeated after several months if necessary.

Instead of **Magnesium carbonica 30**, you might choose to use one tablet of **Magnesium phosphorica 12** three times a day.

If urine "drips" because the bladder is overfilled and expanded beyond its capacity, administer one tablet of **Causticum 6** three times a day.

Inflammation of the Kidneys (Nephritis)

Sudden inflammations of the kidneys occur very rarely in cats. As a result of an accident, a cat's kidneys can be so shaken that they become inflamed. The primary symptom of such an inflammation is blood in the urine.

An acute inflammation of the kidneys requires **Apis 3** or 6 if the urine is held back and **Belladonna 6** if the urine is bloody. Administer these once every hour or two, and less frequently once healing sets in.

In general, chronic inflammations of the kidneys are caused by bacterial poisons in the bloodstream, for example, accumulations of pus from bad teeth or bacteria from inflamed gums. Bacteria from the blood enter into the kidneys and cause damage to them.

The many different types of inflammations of the kidneys are difficult to sort out and have various symptoms. General symptoms to look for are:

- great thirst
- increased output of water-clear urine
- weight loss, especially noticeable around the neck and back
- a sweetish urine-like smell exuding from the oral cavity
- occasional vomiting.

The apathy these animals may experience is related to the fact that they are losing valuable proteins in their urine. In addition, waste products that should be taken care of by the kidneys remain in their bodies and slowly poison them.

Two proven homeopathic remedies should be considered to arrest the development of kidney problems.

The first remedy is one tablet of **Mercurius solubilis** administered three times a day. The urine of the **Mercurius** patient is cloudy and dirty; it contains proteins, it stinks, and it is often mixed with blood even if the blood cannot be seen with the naked eye. The cat experiences pressure and pain in her kidneys, and the surrounding area is very sensitive and painful. Even if all of these symptoms do not appear, **Mercurius** is the remedy of choice in most cases.

The second major remedy is **Arsenicum album**. The **Arsenicum** patient has already begun to lose weight, she tires rapidly, her skin is very dry, and the observant cat-owner can see small scales (large: **Sulphur**) on her hide. She is anxious and restless, changes places often, drinks little but often, and seeks warmth. Her face is sunken, her nose pointed and she appears hollow-eyed. In addition, her vomit smells strongly of dead meat.

The third remedy, **Lespedeza 1**, should be considered if waste products and creatines can be detected in the cat's blood. Your veterinarian can tell you this after performing a few simple tests. This remedy is the last hope and is only helpful if a sufficient portion of the kidney tissues can still function.

If the level of creatines is too high, the cat may experience intestinal difficulties that consistently return despite treatment. Other symptoms to watch for are diarrhea and vomiting, apathy, weight loss, and other vague signs of illness.

With improvement, give the cat one tablet of **Lespedeza 1** three times a day for one week.

From the behavior of the cat one can tell whether these developments can be arrested and whether it is possible to cure a chronically sick kidney.

It is helpful for kidney ailments if you reduce the amount of protein (primarily protein from meat) in the cat's diet to a minimum; give her only as much meat as will encourage her to eat other foods such as dairy products in every form, fat (oil) and carbohydrates, dextrose, and anything else she likes that contains little or no protein.

In order to avoid the dreaded dehydration when the cat does not drink much on her own, you should present her with soupy food that contains a lot of water. But this is seldom necessary.

Improvement is not difficult to discern in the cat's general condition. She will gain weight and she should drink less than before, even when fluids are presented to her.

The cat's intake of fluids must be measured in order to determine whether her condition is improving. Give her one-half to one liter of water in a measuring cup so you have an idea how much she drinks in a day. In this way you ideally will be able to measure her increasing progress.

Constant vomiting, diarrhea, sweetish breath that smells like urine, and abscesses on the mucous membranes of the mouth indicate uremia, the complete breakdown of the kidneys. Uremia can be treated with **Opium 30****, but it cannot be cured.

8

Skin Diseases

Hair and Skin

The fur of a healthy cat should shine in all its colorful glory. If the cat is brushed or combed, some hairs should fall out, but not too few and not too many. The skin should be taut—if you gently pull away a fold of skin, it should snap back elastically. The skin should be warm, not hot, under your hand, and touching the skin should not hurt the cat; she should gladly tolerate it. It would be nice if this were always the case, but even a cat's skin cannot completely escape disease.

Parasites (Fleas, Lice, Ticks)

Infestations of parasites occur often in cats. For example, cats can become infested with fleas while they are chasing mice in the summer grass, or through contact with other infested animals or birds. Fleas are two to three millimeters long, and because they bite the cat, she will constantly scratch the parts of her body preferred by the fleas. Fleas are most commonly found on the cat's neck, back, haunches and around the tail area. Fleas can be carriers of tapeworms if, while trying to rid herself of the fleas, the cat catches and swallows a flea infected with tapeworms.

Mature fleas multiply on the cat since they lay eggs in dark crevices of the house that subsequently hatch into small larvae. After fourteen days, the larvae are large enough to be bothersome to the cat. Therefore, when battling fleas, it is important not to forget to disinfect small corners and chinks in the floor where fleas and their larvae could be hiding. Wash the floors often with a mop or a wet rag and use plenty of floor wax. Also vacuum the carpets more often than usual. It is most effective if you try to find and kill as many of the fleas on the cat as you can. Fleas are easy to recognize; they appear as small black points on the cat's skin.

Severe infestations of fleas can be cured with the help of baths containing antiparasitic preparations, though they may be toxic to the cat and to children who pet them.

You might also try covering the cat with flea powder for fifteen minutes while she is wrapped in a blanket or pillowcase so that only her head peeps out. Afterwards, brush her carefully while holding her over sheets of newspaper. Once you have finished brushing her, promptly roll the newspaper up and throw it away, as fleas do not die immediately.

Internally, it can help your cat if the protective coating of the skin is strengthened and activated with one tablet of **Sulphur 30**, administered once a week for three to four weeks. **Sulphur** chases away fleas and other parasites that may be carriers of bandworms. This treatment also attacks lice.

Tick infestation occurs often in cats that are allowed to venture outside into bushy or wooded areas. The swollen bites itch and are inflamed. Ticks use their snouts to bore into the cat's skin. While the tick is burying itself, it anesthetizes the skin around it so that the cat feels neither the bite nor the sucking of her blood. Ticks make their presence known to an observer only after they have finished sucking up a quantity of blood. At this point they are bloated with blood, and thus very visible.

An elegant method is best for the removal of ticks: because ticks "screw" themselves into the cat counterclockwise, you should be able to take them out with a clockwise turn and pull of your hand. Not the least trace of the tick will remain, not even the head with its pincers. You can also use drops of alcohol, oil, or petroleum to suffocate the tick and then remove it after a few minutes have elapsed. You must only make sure that you get the whole tick and that the head does not remain under the cat's skin; this inevitably leads to skin inflammations.

Small lice can be picked up in hay or straw, in the grass, or from infested animals. Of a whitish-gray color, they can resemble scales on the skin. The preferred places for lice are on the animal's head, neck, and back and also on the end of the tail, especially if the animal has long hair. These blood-suckers multiply with surprising speed and cause the animal to scratch incessantly if they are not controlled. These longish parasites are easily detectable, as are their eggs that stick to the animal's hairs and crackle when you squash them between two thumbnails.

The treatment: Take the cat out of your house or onto the balcony of your apartment and spray her with a readily available flea and tick powder. Afterwards, brush her carefully while holding her over sheets of newspaper. Be sure to promptly roll up the paper and its contents and throw it away. You should repeat this procedure three to four times every seven days, even if it does not seem to be necessary. A flea collar equipped with a flea and tick preparation is a good means of preventing an infestation of parasites on an outdoor cat as long as the collar does not cause a rash on the cat's neck. Indoors, the collar should be removed and kept in a plastic bag since it gives off gases that could be harmful to your health.

Mange

Mange is a relatively rare communicable disease afflicting human beings, cats, and dogs that is caused primarily by ticks. In adult animals, since mange often appears on the head first, it is sometimes called "head-mange." From the head, mange proceeds over the forehead, ears, and eyes to the neck, the paws, and other parts of the body. The skin becomes wrinkled and itches constantly, particularly when the weather is warm. An unpleasant-smelling honey-like coating sometimes appears after moulting.

In young animals, mange occurs first on the stomach and neck. Mangy animals must be isolated if other animals live in the house. The animal's bed, brush, and comb must be disinfected immediately in order to prevent a reinfection with the disease.

The best treatment is to rub the animal with a remedy prescribed by your veterinarian. Normally this must be done at least two or three times a week for two to three weeks.

Homeopathy can only help indirectly by changing the "terrain" of the skin. Healing of the skin is promoted by **Sulphur 6** administered three times a day.

You should discuss other measures with your veterinarian since mange is spread directly from animal to animal. This can, among other things, lead to problems at animal shows.

Fungi

Of all possible fungal diseases, one occurs particularly frequently in cats: ringworm. Ringworm is characterized by round, red patches on the skin that look scaly around their outer edges. These patches occur primarily on the neck and legs but may also occur on the head. The patches may connect with one another and become quite large without appearing especially inflamed. It is also possible that you will notice the formation of crusty scabs. The hairs around the edges of the patches can be pulled out quite easily. Ringworm may be transmitted to human beings if they happen to be susceptible to it. Therefore, treatment should be carried out as quickly and effectively as possible: rub the patches with ether and paint them with iodine. This is the easiest remedy as long as you discover the disease in its early stages, when it has not spread too far.

Release the cat only after the tincture has dried. **Echinacea tincture** is also suitable for treating this condition.

It is recommended that you clip the patches before painting them with iodine. Painting the patches for three to five consecutive days should be sufficient. If necessary, repeat the treatment after a week has elapsed.

Internally, **Sepia** can help cure your cat. Administer three dosages a day for ten days. In case of patches on the skin are larger than an inch and a half in diameter, consult your veterinarian.

Abscesses

Abscesses are easily recognized because they cause local swelling, pain, heat, and the accumulation of pus.

Scratches and rat bites are practically unavoidable in cats that are allowed to go outside at night. When a rat tries to free itself from the cat's grasp, it will almost always bite the cat in the face: old, gray cats are often marked by the scars of many such bites.

Abscesses appear after the cat has been bitten because bite-wounds close up quickly. Abscesses in the throat or under the eye can be caused by the rotten roots of bad teeth; these must be treated by the veterinarian.

If an abscess is warm and sensitive to the touch, administer one dosage of **Hepar sulphuris 3** or **6** every two hours for one to two days. This should solve the problem by causing the abscess to expand and open itself.

Surgical intervention is not necessary; **Hepar sulphuris** is the "homeopathic knife" (another is **Myristica sebifera 3**). The open abscess, once freed of pus, requires a few dosages of **Silicea 12**. Administer **Silicea 12** twice a day for a few days to ensure complete, scar-free healing without additional complications.

If the abscess is cool to the touch, it is a "cold abscess" that causes the cat hardly any pain. Administer **Silicea 12** three times a day for several days.

If it should become necessary to open the abscess with a knife, the cut must not be too small because cuts grow back together very rapidly.

Acne and Pustules

The pimple-disease is caused by bacteria that enter the hair follicles and form pustules or knots. The pustules are filled with pus or a watery fluid and can often be found on the head and chest. The remedy is **Hepar sulphuris 12**.

If many knots are present, **Silicea 12** can help. It melts the knots away after a treatment lasting between eight and fourteen days.

Acne can also be the result of a hormonal imbalance related to disturbances in the heat cycle. In this case, it is a good idea to have the cat sterilized; sterilized cats rarely suffer from acne.

Digestive difficulties can also cause acne. If this seems to be the case, try changing the cat's diet.

Eczema

Eczema is an inflammation of the skin. It is caused by various internal and external factors such as parasites and fungi, chronic stomach or intestinal problems, an imbalance in the diet, disturbances in the metabolism, allergies or even diabetes.

At the beginning, try to eliminate as many possible causes as you can! Treat the cat for parasite infestation and watch her diet carefully.

Non-parasitic eczema can take a number of forms:

Damp eczema

Damp eczema is found primarily in the hollows of joints, accompanied by sticky secretions and a rather rotten smell. It requires **Graphites 6**.

These animals are overfed and too fat, they are lazy, sleep a lot, and never refuse anything that resembles food.

Wet eczema

Wet eczema tends to be reddish, with inflamed skin; it can be treated successfully with **Mercurius solubilis 6**.

Scabby eczema

Scabby eczema can be treated with **Mezereum 6** in alternation with **Petroleum 6**.

Eczema that proceeds with torn, open, swollen skin

Typical for this condition are cracks and moist eruptions on the areas between the skin and mucous membranes (the areas around the nose, the ears, the anus). These symptoms become worse during the colder parts of the year. This condition may be cured with **Petroleum 6**.

Dry eczema—Type #1

This type of dry eczema is characterized by pale, cloudy skin that itches and burns, flaky scalp, hair that is falling out, and small scales like dust. This dry, often chronic eczema requires **Arsenicum album 6.**

The **Arsenicum** patient drinks often, but only a little at a time. This condition becomes worse at night and better in warmer places. These are cats that would crawl not only on top of, but actually into, the oven—that is, if people still had houses heated with large ovens.

Dry eczema—Type #2

This type of dry eczema has dirty, reddish skin, foul-smelling discharge, and relatively large scales. It requires **Sulphur 6** as a remedy, especially if the cat's body openings (the conjunctiva around the eyes, the oral cavity, the inner ear, the area around the anus) are redder than normal.

In addition, defecation is often disturbed. At first, the feces are too hard, then later in the same stool, they are too soft. These patients avoid warmth and prefer to remain where it is cool—precisely because they feel too hot!

Eczema that is often infected

This type of eczema can occur on the claws—the skin between the toes is swollen and the cat licks it often. This condition calls for **Silicea 6** for a lengthy period of time until it is cured.

Induration of the Skin

Swellings of the skin or wounds caused by the constant scratching-off of scars that have a hard, thickened area underneath them (often these are to be found on the neck) should be treated with **Silicea 30**. Administer **Silicea 30** three times a day for four to eight days. Scratching should subside, the swellings of the skin should disappear, and the skin will become normal once again.

Naturally it is helpful if you can put a bandage on the afflicted area while it is healing, but do this only if the cat will tolerate it.

Maggot Infestation

Flies sometimes lay their eggs on a dirty patch around the anus or vagina of a weak or sick cat. The eggs rapidly develop into maggots that, in the truest sense of the word, eat the cat alive. Immediate care by the veterinarian is imperative. If the infestation is discovered late and maggots have already entered the cat's anus or vagina, it is difficult to save her.

You should rid the cat of maggots immediately by cleaning the hair and skin around the afflicted areas with a disinfecting agent. It is also possible to use chloroform to kill the maggots.

Matting or Tufting of the Hair (Trichosis)

If a cat's hair tufts, a lack of care taken by the cat is only partially responsible. The matting begins behind the ears and can spread over the cat's entire coat so that a brush or comb is useless.

The cause of this condition is a calcium imbalance. After you trim off the matted tufts of hair (a process some cats will tolerate only if they are anesthetized), the hair should grow back normally if the correct remedy is administered for three weeks.

In most cases, the best remedy is one dosage of **Calcarea fluorica 12** administered twice a day.

Hair Loss

Hair loss in cats can have various causes. Naturally the seasons play a role. When winter is over, every cat "takes off" her winter coat. This process cannot be avoided.

In case of heavy hair loss throughout the year, try administering two dosages of **Phosphoric acid 6** daily for fourteen days. **Thallium 10** or **12**, administered in the same manner, has also proven helpful.

If a cat is fed only canned food and hair loss is particularly pronounced on her joints, the underside of her stomach, and when she is stroked, consider **Natrum muriaticum 12** three times a day.

If hair loss is due to hormonal causes—for example it is worse after heat—then young animals should be given **Lachesis 12** and older ones **Sepia 12** twice a day for ten to fourteen days.

Hair Breakage

Hair breakage occurs in all kinds of cats regardless of their sex: the beard-hair breaks, and later the under-wool falls out—frequently first on the withers.

This disturbance is caused by damage to the liver. It is difficult to diagnose in the laboratory and can be cured with **Lycopodium 30** administered once a day for ten days. If this treatment is unsuccessful, repeat it one more time after three weeks.

Loss of Whiskers

If a cat should lose her whiskers, the cause is stress. **Kali phosphorica 12** is the recommended remedy.

Dandruff

The formation of scales is not a disease, but for the alert cat-owner it should be a sign of the beginning of a metabolic disturbance.

Much can be achieved with a change of diet—most importantly, give the cat no dry food for a time—and brush her coat regularly. The formation of scales on warm, reddish skin requires **Sulphur 6.** If there are very small, almost dust-like scales on pale, dry skin, give **Arsenicum album 6.** Administer the correct remedy twice a day for ten days.

Abnormal Secretion of Sebum (Seborrhiasis)

So-called "fatty-tail," which is visible on the top side of the base of the cat's tail, is the product of excessive secretion of sebum. This condition is frequently found in young animals.

Internally: administer three dosages of **Calcarea carbonica 6** daily.

Externally: powder the cat with potato-flour, or wash with witchhazel, dry, and pat in corn starch.

Reactions to Vaccinations

Because in the last few years cats have been given more and more inoculations, it is possible that a cat can exhibit an allergic reaction to a particular injection. Such reactions make their presence known either immediately after the inoculation or sometimes only after a few days have elapsed.

Local swellings of the skin may occur in the area where the injection was given. Then, **Thuja 12** (or another **Thuja** potency if it is more readily available) is the correct remedy. A few dosages should cure the cat quickly.

If the reaction to an injection is not local but general, in that the cat lies around apathetically, administer two or three dosages of **Silicea 12** daily for several days.

9

Dangerous Viruses and Bacteria

Like all living things, cats are vulnerable to the effects of viruses and bacteria that can have very serious consequences.

Feline Distemper

Every cat-owner knows the meaning of the dreaded words "feline distemper."

Feline distemper is a general term for various viral illnesses that can attack the stomach and intestinal tract as well as the mucous membranes of the throat. It is often difficult to diagnose, even for an expert. The term "panleukopenia" has been adopted because all of these forms have in common the breakdown of the leucocytes (white corpuscles) in the blood. In a blood profile, a drop in the number of white cells, the "blood-police," becomes obvious. Resistance mechanisms are blocked, secondary infections crop up, and death can follow within five days, or in extreme cases, within twenty-four hours.

Feline distemper occurs most frequently in the autumn in cats under two years of age. The sick animal is the very picture of misery. Vomiting occurs at the beginning, often so violent that you might be inclined to suspect a poisoning or a foreign body in the stomach. The cat may have a fever of up to 106 degrees Fahrenheit, accompanied by viscous greenish-yellow mucus that is vomited up with great effort. The cat's breath stinks and every now and then she may have diarrhea that can be watery or bloody-slimy.

The cat's body becomes extremely dehydrated due to the loss of fluids. The rim of the tongue is inflamed and may be swollen as well. Drooling, the cat sits apathetically before her food dish and would like very much to eat, but cannot.

This is the hour of **Baptisia!** **Baptisia 3** or **30**—in whatever potency the pharmacy happens to have it—can work miracles here. The cat's general condition should improve rapidly. **Baptisia** should be administered every two hours on the first day, then three times a day until the cat's appetite returns.

It will help the cat if you feed her small meatballs through the corners of her mouth—in this manner she can eat without moving her tongue.

Once again: **Baptisia** is the trump here. It helps reliably as long as the disease has taken hold in the upper part of the cat's body. If diarrhea is the primary symptom, it indicates that the lower part of the cat's body is infected. In this case, administer **Mercurius corrosivus** in the potency **6** or **30** every two hours on the first day, then with increasing improvement, three times a day until the cat is cured.

With these two homeopathic remedies, you have a handle on treatment of the two most common variations of feline distemper. If no complications arise, you can hope for quick and complete healing. Prophylactic inoculations are no longer necessary after an attack of feline distemper because the cat becomes immune to this disease.

It is not necessary to discuss other viral illnesses here because they seldom occur in cats, and exactly because they seldom occur, no homeopathic treatment has been developed for them.

This also holds true for Feline Infectious Peritonitis (FIP), an infectious inflammation of the stomach tissues, and for pseudo-rabies, and infectious anemia.

Toxoplasmosis

If cats are very sick with toxoplasmosis, they defecate little cysts (oocysts). The cat's feces need to be removed daily.

If the feces are not removed, the little cysts dry up on the surface of the feces and can be transmitted to human beings in the form of particles in the air. Not only human beings, but also dogs, pigs, sheep, goats, and other animals can be affected. Every animal eaten by people is susceptible to toxoplasmosis and can transmit the disease to those humans who eat raw meat.

The actual illness is not terribly severe or noticeable in human beings; as in cats, toxoplasmosis can seem similar to a grippe that lasts a long time and from which the patient only slowly recovers. Statistics tell us that the degree of latent infection climbs from 30–50% in younger people to 50–70% in people over seventy years of age. It is only dangerous to pregnant women, however.

The profile of toxoplasmosis in cats appears much like the profile of a cold. It normally runs its course quietly and maybe even unknown to the cat-owner. But the exception proves the rule: inflammations of the lungs, liver, and the membrane covering the brain caused by toxoplasmosis have been described.

Diagnosis of toxoplasmosis is difficult, as you need blood samples that are not easy to extract from the tender veins of a cat. The two forms of proof, the Sabin-Feldmann test and the complementary action test, will both come back positive in case of an acute illness. The positive Sabin-Feldmann test alone only indicates the presence of a well-established illness. Homeopathic treatment of toxoplasmosis in animals proceeds exactly as it does in human beings: the resistance is strengthened with one tablet of **Echinacea 1** administered three times a day for several weeks, and the toxoplasmosis is "neutralized" with **Nosode toxoplasmose 15*** administered once a day, also for several weeks.

The progress of the disease is evident in repeated blood samples. This holds true even for relatively symptom-free toxoplasmosis. In case of accompanying illnesses, the correct remedy for each illness must be sought out and administered along with the remedies for toxoplasmosis.

Rabies

While I was still a student, a veterinarian in East Prussia told me about an attack of rabies there: a small fox came upon some children at play. The fox seemed very tame; he even allowed the children to pick him up and play with him. Later, the children tucked the fox into their doll-carriage and took him for a walk. Finally, an adult noticed that something was wrong and called the local forester. The forester took the fox into the laboratory for testing. After several days, the news came back: the fox was rabid.

Rabies inoculations were unknown in those days. Luckily, nothing happened to the children. If they are still alive, they must be grandparents and tell their grandchildren this story when the subject of rabies comes up. The fact that not all human beingsbecome infected with rabies, even if they are bitten, has long been known.

How does rabies look in a cat?

The symptoms are not uniform. Cats tend more towards

"quiet" rabies in the sense that a cat infected with rabies by the bite of a rabid animal will often appear "healthy" for a long time.

Visible changes in the cat's behavior occur with the progression of the disease. Before she reaches the final stage, the cat will lose all fear, be easily excitable, shun light and water, be irritated by noise and movement, and since she will not be able to swallow, she will drool. Her lower jaw, larynx, and pharynx may also be lamed. In addition, she may limp first on one leg, then on both hind legs, due to increasing weakness in her hindquarters that can lead to paralysis of the entire body. If the rabies does not progress so "quietly," you may notice cramps, the cat may attack people, scratch and bite them (especially in the face), and be exceedingly aggressive. The lameness-stage will quickly follow. First the cat may have trouble swallowing, then she will be almost completely paralyzed.

Because no reliable cure is known and the government will not tolerate attempts at treatment, the inoculation of domestic animals in rabies-infested areas is the best protection against rabies. Inoculations are required by most countries if you wish to take your cat on vacation with you.

10

Poisonings

Poisonings may occur through the stomach, the skin or the lungs. They happen because of ill-will, lack of attention on the part of the cat-owner, or mix-ups. Poisonings are caused by harmful vegetable, animal, or chemical substances.

Plants that are poisonous for cats include: amaryllis, primroses, carnations, geraniums, snowdrops, lilies-of-the-valley, crocuses, hyacinths, anemones, narcissus, laburnam, wild violets, magnolia, ferns, cacti, and many others.

Chemical substances: improper or too much flea powder; pesticides, paint and paint and lacquer-removers; all cleaning and polishing agents and bleaches; suntan oil, color-solvents, hair spray, dyes, glues, carpet glues, antifreeze and all waxing and polishing agents for floors or furniture that contain petroleum distillates—in general almost every chemical that can be found in an average household.

Luckily, the eating habits of most cats prevent them from consuming much of most poisonous substances; cats eat slowly and carefully, not quickly and greedily like dogs do. Cats chew their food sufficiently and taste it enough to be able to refuse it if they do not like it.

A cat's curiosity, on the other hand, is a disadvantage. She is likely to try out every new flower in the house and follow her hunting instincts even if it means chasing and eating a mouse that has been poisoned. The way cats clean themselves also leaves them open to the possibility of poisoning. If insecticides or harmful substances stick to a cat's fur, she is likely to ingest them when she licks herself clean. In this case, poisoning is practically unavoidable.

Poisonings can only be diagnosed with certainty if the cat-owner knows what has happened and has observed the progression of symptoms.

Vague symptoms that do not fit any particular diagnosis may be an indication of a poisoning, especially if the illness comes out of the blue and proceeds with vomiting, diarrhea (possibly bloody), weight loss, and extreme sensitivity of the lower part of the body. All poisonings have one thing in common: they cause no fever if they do not proceed with cramps.

In case of a suspected poisoning, **Okoubaka**** 2 or 3 work well as antidotes (**Okoubaka** is not an officially recognized homeopathic medicine in the United States. In its place, a cat owner should consider **Arsenicum, Nux vomica,** or **Ipecac** in the 6th potency).

Because most poisons work quickly and you seldom know for sure what kinds of harmful substances they contain, you should give the cat **Okoubaka**** 2 or 3 every fifteen minutes until improvement is noticeable, then less frequently until you have reached the veterinarian's office. This African bark is worth its weight in gold if you need to neutralize poisons of any sort ingested with the food. You should keep a supply of **Okoubaka** at home or make sure there is a good pharmacy nearby.

Each piece of evidence pointing to a poisoning is valuable to the veterinarian since the treatment he chooses depends on the symptoms present. Therefore, take everything with you that could be a cause—leftovers of food, prey the cat has eaten, medicines and boxes, bottles, glasses, and anything else suspicious.

Of the many possibilities, let only a few be mentioned: In the case of an insecticide poisoning, the cat will drool, have diarrhea, and tremble. Trembling can eventually lead to cramps. In addition, the cat may have problems with her balance and coordination and be exceedingly anxious.

The quick removal of all traces of poison from the cat's skin with soap and water is a critical measure.

In case an emetic is necessary, do not use castor oil since many poisons dissolve particularly well in oil. Instead, put an enema containing a children's laxative (available at most pharmacies) into the cat's anus. In case of severe cramps, the veterinarian will inject a sedative and dextrose as an antidote for poisons.

If constant vomiting occurs after a chemical treatment with sulfonamides that borders on a poisoning, or in case of an overdose of antibiotics, **Ipecacuanha 6** administered once an hour can be of great help.

In case of a poisoning with rat poison that interferes with the flow of blood, hemorrhages often occur. The mucous membranes become pale and seem bluish. This symptom is accompanied by bloody vomiting, bloody defecation, bloody urine, blood in the chest cavity—everything is bleeding.

Here, Vitamin K is the specific remedy. This should be supplemented with an injection of one ampule of **Phosphorus 30** and one ampule of a heart and circulatory remedy (**Cactus 1**, **Crataegus 1***, **Veratrum 3**). Your veterinarian should be responsible for this treatment.

11

Cleanliness Habits
and Other Problems

During the weaning of her kittens, the mother cat teaches them the basic principles of cleanliness. By the time they are six weeks old, all kittens should be able to use the litter box. If a cat is not box-trained by this time, experience shows that she never will be. Inbreeding and a lack of intelligence can play a role here, as can inborn sensory defects that defy all kinds of treatment.

If mature cats suddenly become unclean and defecate in places other than the litter box, there can be various reasons: If a female cat urinates a little here and a little there, she is probably in heat. Uncastrated male cats mark out their territory with sprays of urine or feces after they reach sexual maturity. This has nothing to do with "neurosis," but instead is a natural method of marking out territory that is particular to cats.

However, many causes can be psychological: If a cat's desires are not quenched, her usual habits are interrupted for one reason or another, or conflicts with other cats arise— only to name a few reasons—this can lead to uncleanliness.

Because this represents an "unloading-reaction," it can become a problem. There are several possibilities for homeopathic treatment. Before these are put into practice, however, you should give some thought to what the causes might be and try to eliminate as many of them as you can.

If grief, vexation, or neglect are possible causes, attempt treatment with one tablet of **Ignatia 30** three times on one day and then no more. If it is indeed the correct remedy, the condition of the animal should improve by the next day. **Ignatia** is effective as a homeopathic "homesickness-remedy," in case of a change of location, or even if a cat loses a particularly dear human being or animal-friend.

If the furniture in a room is moved around, a cat can become so frustrated that she will become unclean. In this case, try three dosages of **Argentum nitricum 12** daily until improvement is noticeable. This remedy should restore the cat's psychological balance.

A great shock can cause uncleanliness, for example if the cat is chased as if for life and death. Then, the cat needs **Opium 30****.

The same remedy is good for after-effects of anesthesia, for example if anesthesia causes changes in the cat's system. Luckily, this occurs rarely. Administer **Opium 30****.

Rivalries between two or more cats living in the same household can be treated with one single dosage of **Chamomilla 200**. All "fighting patients" should be given the remedy at the same time, regardless of whether or not rivalries have led to uncleanliness.

If a cat becomes unclean after an inoculation, **Thuja 12** administered twice a day for several days can help.

If an old cat, generally clean, forgets where her litter box is—the observant cat-owner can easily make this diagnosis—then two dosages of **Baryta carbonica 6** daily for several days can solve this problem.

And for the physical causes of uncleanliness: If the cat cannot hold her urine after being soaked to the skin or after a bath, **Dulcamara 6** or **Rhus toxicodendron 6** or 12 is the correct remedy.

If the cat urinates unconsciously while she is asleep, **Petroselinum 6** can help.

Weakness in old age of the muscles that close the bladder can be treated with **Causticum 12**. Weakness of the anus should be treated with **Aloe 6**.

If a recent or even not-so-recent traumatic event is the cause of uncleanliness (for example, a fall from a window, an accident, etc.), administer one dosage of **Arnica 30** daily until improvement is noticeable.

You should rid cats that bite, especially those that bite your legs, of their apparently aggressive nature by playing with them often. Use a mouse-like toy on a string and pull it by the cat. Other good toys are wads of paper or corks with feathers stuck in them. Such games satisfy the cat's desire to hunt. If, however, a cat frequently bites the people around her without apparent cause, then she is really afraid and overcompensating for her fear. The remedy for this condition is **Belladonna 30**. Administer one dosage daily for seven to ten days. In this context it can happen that the cat will become unclean because of her fear, and she will defecate and urinate in hidden places where she should not and where she earlier did not.

This **Belladonna** cat has an unnatural sensitivity to light and noise. After an anger-attack she cannot sleep, and when she finally does fall asleep, she sighs and snarls and grinds her teeth.

There is yet another form of the biting and scratching routine that appears frequently in female Siamese cats: the cat will allow you to stroke her, she purrs and seems to be truly happy. In the next moment, however, she scratches and bites so that the fur flies. The smallest annoyance causes anger and a bad mood—perhaps for hours!

Here, the remedy is **Platina 30.** The **Platina** cat is egocentric, proud, and presumptuous; she looks down on the world.

These cats are oversexed and constantly hungry. Typically, if these cats are in a strange place (on a trip) or they do not have their usual food dish, they will not defecate. They are constipated and urinate more frequently and in greater quantities than usual.

Obesity

Because of castration or sterilization, a break occurs in a cat's hormonal system that can even out her temperament and weight gain.

While the former change is usually welcome, weight gain can become a problem if it progresses and the cat becomes obese. If a castration or sterilization is performed too early, obesity is the likely consequence. And obesity can easily become a disease.

The extra pounds overburden the heart, the circulatory system and all other internal organs. For this reason, you should take weight gain seriously—and do everything you can to prevent it.

The normal weight of an adult cat is between two and a half and five kilograms (5 to 11 pounds). Cats that weigh five kilograms are considered to be within the normal range if they have exceptionally large, strong bones. Any cat that weighs more than five kilograms is overweight.

It would be nice and easy for many cat-owners if there were a homeopathic remedy for weight gain. There are indeed homeopathic remedies for obesity, but only when obesity is caused by problems with the thyroid gland (administer one dosage of **Thyroidinum 30** daily)—this occurs so rarely that you should forget about it. No, it is mostly poor feeding habits, often also a bad attitude on the part of the cat-owner, who overfeeds his cat in an attempt to do her a favor.

The cat-owner should think about providing low-calorie foods such as vegetables and lean meat for his cat.

If this is not enough to make the cat lose weight, then you should feed the cat one-fifth less food than normal for ten days. If no result is obvious, feed the cat two-fifths less food than normal until you can see that she has lost some weight.

Only a cat-owner who is firmly convinced that he is doing something good and life-lengthening for his cat can initiate and follow through with such a cure.

The same routine goes for prepared cat food. Give the cat one-fifth less food than usual, but do this only if the cat is used to prepared food. If she has been fed something else in the past, you would have to change her food gradually, then subsequently reduce the amount in order to begin the reduction of the cat's caloric intake.

All of this is tiresome!

Here, the old saying that "an ounce of prevention is worth a pound of cure" certainly holds true.

12

The Old Cat

Like human beings, cats have been living longer in recent years. On the average, cats live about twelve years; with good care, however, they can live to be as old as sixteen to twenty years.

You might be wondering whether with the help of homeopathic remedies, a cat's life can be extended.

It is hard to say whether or not the regular administration of homeopathic remedies can help cats live longer because no one knows exactly when a cat's time is up. Certainly the correct remedies can help keep your cat healthy and happy and prevent the onset of serious illness in old age.

The cat's heart and liver are the organs most prone to failure in old age; you should ensure that her circulation remains strong thanks to a healthy heart muscle!

It is just as important that you stimulate the cat's kidneys so they will continue to function properly. Prophylactic care concentrates primarily on the kidneys in order to prevent the untimely development of sight and hearing problems.

Arnica 200 should be given once every seven days to cats that have slowed down significantly. They are tired and apathetic, and may fall over from time to time. **Arnica** ensures that circulation remains strong.

Mercurius 200 given every seven days is for cats that drink a lot. The intake of more fluids than usual indicates kidney damage.

Calcarea carbonica 12: One dosage daily for several weeks can help cats that have become fat and slow in old age and show signs of developing cataracts.

Calcarea fluorica 12: Administer one dosage for cats that have developed tufts in their fur, have begun to lose weight, and have cataracts. Administer for three weeks a quarter (13 weeks).

Baryta carbonica 6 is given twice a day for cats that forget where their litter box is from time to time and therefore become unclean. These cats frequently have skin problems.

Cerebral Hemorrhage

Cerebral hemorrhages occur seldom in cats. When they do, they come in the form of strokes and are the result of a hardening of the arteries of a very old cat. According to the severity of the hemorrhage, the cat may experience motor difficulties—for example, she may run in circles or be lamed on one side of her body.

In case of a sudden stroke, homeopathy has two proven remedies. These remedies work equally well in human beings and animals and should be administered immediately after the stroke! Use **Arnica 3** and **Belladonna 6** in alternation every fifteen minutes. Place five drops directly on the cat's tongue. Increase the interval between dosages once improvement is noticeable. The first day is especially important!

This preparation works very quickly in curable cases—as **Baptisia** also does. Both the cat-owner and the veterinarian will be amazed.

Changes in the Bones in Old Age

Changes in a cat's bones due to the effects of old age go largely undetected. Most of the symptoms such as the inflammation of the vertebrae (spondylitis), osteoporosis, or the loss of calcium from the bones can only be revealed with the help of x-rays. These symptoms react, insofar as they cause disturbances in movement, to one dosage of **Calcarea fluorica 3** or **6** daily for several weeks.

13

First Aid

Accidents

In case of accidents, falls from windows and all consequences of impact, beatings, or other injuries:

Arnica in every potency, but especially 6, can help. At first, administer one dosage every fifteen minutes. As of the fourth dosage, administer every thirty minutes if possible. If the cat is still obviously ill, wrap her in a blanket or pack her in a transport basket and take her immediately to the nearest veterinarian.

Staunch bleeding from an artery with a pressure bandage and take the cat directly to the veterinarian, as wounds that bleed a lot nearly always require stitches.

Arnica can also help in cases of shock, failure of the circulatory system, and severe bleeding (you may also use a preparation that contains Arnica).

Even if the cat is unconscious, you should crush a tablet and apply it to the mucous membranes of her mouth where it will be absorbed quickly and enter her bloodstream. Naturally this is easier with drops, but because they contain alcohol, the cat will be reluctant to consume them.

Treatment of Wounds

The differentiation of symptoms is important for the homeopathic treatment of wounds:

Contusions that occur in cats if they fall (this does happen!) and the head bleeds call for **Arnica 6** together with **Hamamelis 3** administered internally. You may also wish to apply a bandage with Calendula salve.

Surgical wounds that heal badly: if, for example, lymphatic fluid accumulates after the sterilization of a cat, **Staphysagria 6** is the remedy. This may be followed up with **Graphites** and **Silicea**. Cut-wounds, like those that come about due to an operation, should be treated with **Arnica 30** once the operation is over. Administer one tablet every four hours for three days in order to avoid complications in the healing process. A wonderful remedy!

If scars leak pus or grow out of control, you should consider **Staphysagria 6**. So-called *scar keloids* dissolve when treated with **Silicea 6** and **Fluoric acid 12** should keloids develop.

Bite wounds that involve a loss of tissue require **Calendula** salve externally and three daily dosages of five drops each of **Calendula 3** internally.

Skin abrasions that occur near nerve endings call for **Hypericum tincture** externally and **Hypericum 6** internally.

Puncture or bite wounds (from insects or pointed objects) require **Ledum 6**. In fact, **Ledum 6** is good for all sorts of punctures, including those from needles or rat-bites. Infections resulting from the punctures will also be cured.

Injuries to the tendons, ligaments and joints are well cared for with **Ruta graveolens 6** internally and **Calendula** poultices externally.

Scratch and Bite Wounds

Skin injuries due to encounters with rats, mice, dogs or other cats are not uncommon.

If bacteria penetrate the outer layers of skin, a cellulitis, or flat, pus-filled inflammation of the cell tissues can occur. A cellulitis proceeds with swelling, pain and a marked deterioration of the cat's general condition; it is often accompanied by a fever. Such a condition—in general the domain of antibiotics—reacts well to **Lachesis 12** administered every three hours. In severe cases, administer **Echinacea 1** and **Pyrogenium 15** as well.

Burns

Every now and then a cat may burn herself on the stove or in some other way.

For fast-acting, successful treatment, a poultice with warm 70–90% alcohol is highly recommended. You should place a piece of cloth soaked in warm alcohol on the wound and put a bandage over it. For mild burns, leave the poultice on for one hour. For severe burns, leave it on for as long as twelve hours. After you take the bandage off, if you can still see traces of the burn, apply **Calendula** salve or **Hypericum** tincture.

This treatment can really be called homeopathic because similarity is cured with the similar in the truest sense. Internally, **Echinacea 1** can regenerate damaged skin if you administer it two to three times a day for several days in the cat's food.

Concussions

A fall or other accident can cause a concussion. Mild concussions are frequently overlooked because the cat staggers for a moment, then falls over, but since she gets up immediately, it is as if nothing happened.

Severe concussions can cause vomiting and unconsciousness that last a long time—if they do not lead to death by way of a cerebral hemorrhage. The cat's eyeballs roll wildly from side to side or are fixed in the direction of her nose. In addition, she may breathe heavily and deeply, urinate or defecate, and her pupils may be open very wide. Especially if her pupils are open wide, the cat should be placed in a quiet place near her owner in her basket so that he can administer the necessary remedies even if she is unconscious.

You should not hesitate; you should administer **Arnica 3** and **Hypericum 3** in alternation, at first every fifteen minutes for two hours, then later once every hour until improvement is noticeable.

If deep sleep or unconsciousness lasts too long, give the cat one dosage of **Opium 30**** every hour until she awakens. According to the severity of the injury, this can help.

Victims of seemingly "good" falls and cats that have survived accidents with only minor injuries should receive **Arnica** as well for several days to ensure healing without complications. In such cases, **Arnica** fulfills a prophylactic function in that it prevents the formation of scar tissue in the brain which can lead to changes in the cat's nature and behavior.

Operations

In preparation for an operation, **Arnica** has proven itself useful for avoiding heavy bleeding and minimizing shock. It should be administered three times a day for two days before the operation.

After the operation, **Arnica** is even more important: you should administer **Arnica 30** three times a day for three days.

You may be amazed how lively the cat is on the next day; she will behave as if nothing at all had happened to her. Bandages are not necessary because the cat will not lick the area around the stitches. Healing should be rapid and painless. These are true miracles in everyday life!

Insect Bites

The symptoms of a bee or wasp sting should be treated with homeopathically prepared bee poison. The recommended remedy is **Apis 3** administered every fifteen minutes. Give the cat about five dosages and put a cold cloth on the area around the sting.

Heatstroke

No healthy cat sits in the sun for too long. In hot weather, cats seek out shady places. Heatstroke can only occur in a parked car standing in the hot sun. Typical symptoms are the collapse of the circulatory system, accompanied by heavy breathing, dizzy spells, and a high rectal temperature. Externally, bathe the cat in cold water or wrap her in a cloth containing ice cubes. Internally, administer **Belladonna 6** every fifteen minutes four or five times.

Blood Loss

Cuts or knife-wounds that are not too large should stop bleeding after a few minutes. In case of larger wounds, apply a pressure bandage.

Electric Shock

Cats will occasionally shock themselves while playing around electric outlets. Naturally the first thing you should do is turn the electricity off! Do not try to pull the cat away with your bare hands. Do this only wearing rubber gloves.

Lay an unconscious cat on her side and begin artificial respiration: pull her tongue out, stretch her neck out and press gently on her rib cage with the flat of your hand so that the air can flow out of the lungs and then back in. Repeat until successful at intervals of two to four seconds.

Drowning

Most cats do not like water, but they are naturally good swimmers. Sometimes, however, a cat will find herself unable to climb out of a pond or pool into which she has fallen. You should grasp a drowning cat in the water by the scruff of the neck, then hold her by her hind legs and swing her a few times in a circle so that her respiratory tract is freed of water. Afterwards, lay her on her side and begin artificial respiration if necessary.

14

Repertory of Remedies

Abrotanum: For roundworm, weight loss despite good appetite, diarrhea in alternation with constipation.

Aconitum: For the first stages of a fever on the rise. The fever is released by dry cold. This acute fever is accompanied by a diarrhea, extreme palpitations of the heart, rapid breathing, and anxious restlessness with a hot, red head. The symptoms get worse in the evening, which means that the attentive cat-owner must call the veterinarian late at night. The phase of illness that can be treated with **Aconitum** is very short. **Aconitum** should be followed by **Belladonna** or **Bryonia**, for **Aconitum** cannot help any more if the inflammation has localized itself in an organ. An important remedy to keep in your home pharmacy for the first phase of every kind of fever.

Apis: For inflammations, specifically those of the kidneys and bladder. **Apis** should cause urination.

Arnica: For all results of influences such as impact, beatings, falls, accidents, operations, all traumas, overworked hearts.

Arsenicum album: For dry eczema, diarrhea that smells cadaverous and begins at night, caused by spoiled food. Infections of the intestines, chronic kidney complaints with weight loss. **Arsenicum** is only indicated if you notice anxiety and restlessness—for example, frequent changing of place—and deterioration after midnight. The patient drinks often, but only a little. The skin is dry and itches, and you should be able to see small scales (Sulphur: big scales).

Baptisia: For feline leukemia, localized in the nose-throat-mouth area; the rim of the tongue is swollen. The patient sits in front of her food dish and will not eat.

Belladonna: For local inflammations, wide pupils, racing pulse and hot skin. Deterioration after baths or clipping. Muscle cramps, anxiety. Is indicated in cases that deteriorate because of light, sound, vibration or touch.

Berberis: A liver and kidney remedy. Urinary calculus, inflammation of the bladder with blood in the urine. Pressure on the loin-muscles hurts. Drainage remedy for fat cats.

Bryonia: For bronchitis, inflammation of the lungs, pleurisy. Deteriorates with movement. Improves with quiet rest. The patient lies on the sick side, the lame leg, because pressure feels good. Deterioration with heat. Constipation due to dehydration of the mucous membranes. The patient drinks a lot at one time.

Calcarea carbonica: Made from the insides of oyster shells, this remedy regulates the calcium balance in bones and muscles, especially in very young or old patients. Babies are top-heavy, overweight and slow.

Calcarea fluorica: Regulates the consistency and hardness of bones and teeth. Also important for the skin and hair. A powerful remedy.

Calcarea phosphorica: For cats who are noticeably thinner and more lively in temperament. Has bearing on the growth of bones and teeth.

Calendula: Good for wounds, pinch-wounds, excellent salve for all types of wounds.

Cantharis: For bladder and kidney complaints with bloody urine and intense pressure.

Carbo vegetabilis: For disturbances in the intestine, buildup of gas in the intestine, foul mouth odor.

Carduus marianus: Remedy for the liver, hookworms.

Conium: Blockage of the glands or tumors.

China: Good for consequences of intestinal inflammations accompanied by weakness and exhaustion.

Drosera: For mucous membranes of the upper respiratory tract. Nightly coughing fits with tendency to vomit. Convulsive coughing.

Echinacea: Strengthens the body's resistance after injuries or in case of inflammatory illnesses.

Euphrasia: For conjunctiva, illnesses of the eyes.

Ferrum phosphorica: A remedy for fever.

Helonias: Treats inflammation of the uterus, tonic for the uterus.

Hepar sulphuris: For fear of being touched, constant pustules on the skin or mucous membranes. This patient is prone to catch colds and other illnesses, "falls" from one illness to another. Remedy for abscesses.

Hydrastis: A remedy for mucous membranes, secretion is thick and yellow.

Hypericum: A remedy for nerves, especially if the loin area is extremely sensitive to touch. Good for wounds with nerve endings lying bare. Excellent external application for burns and lacerations.

Ignatia: A remedy for homesickness and when the cat is grieving.

Ipecacuanha: For vomiting accompanied by diarrhea, bronchitis and illnesses of the upper respiratory tract.

Lachesis: For septic processes, blood poisoning, high fever, inflammation of the uterus.

Lycopodium: A liver remedy. A primary symptom is extreme hunger that is satisfied with only a few bites. Smelly urine with a reddish color.

Mercurius solubilis: For the treatment of degenerative cells (kidney, eyeball), swelling of the gums accompanied by light bleeding. Worse in the time between sundown and sunup.

Natrum muriaticum: An excellent remedy for sodium deficiencies caused by prepared food; accompanied by hair loss and a tendency towards eczema.

Nux vomica: A stomach and intestinal remedy in case of poor appetite and constipation with suspicious pressure, flatulence with colic, or after spoiled food. Achieves a cleansing effect in the stomach and intestinal tract.

Okoubaka**: A remedy for alimentary poisoning.

Phosphorus: A remedy for hemorrhages of the mucous membranes and bloody diarrhea, but also inflammation of the lungs, glaucoma.

Phytolacca: Good for swelling of the teats, the development of "knots" after heat.

Pulsatilla: Treats diarrhea after food that is too cold, caused by meat from the refrigerator. Illness of the mucous membranes of the stomach, of the conjunctiva, or the uterus.

Pyrogenium: For feverish infections that develop slowly, not as stormy as **Lachesis**.

Rhus toxicodendron: For joints, muscles, tendon, ligaments. Sprains, tears, inflammations of the tendons. Deteriorates with quiet rest, improves with movement.

Sepia: For ovaries and uterus. Herpes tonsurans.

Silicea: For pus-filled pustules of a chronic nature, thickening of the skin, scar formation.

Sticta pulmonaria: Sooths mucous membranes of the upper respiratory tract, tortuous coughing, chronic sinusitis.

Sulphur: Enhances the reaction and extraction of poison. This emetic will remove harmful substances from the system—including poisons resulting from chemical treatment. One dosage of Sulphur 30 is enough. It is the remedy that may be given once after the conclusion of a treatment to ensure the condition that was treated does not return. Also useful when the patient is shedding.

Thuja: For polyps in the nasal cavity, proliferation of new growths in the ear canal.

IMPORTANT NOTE: There are numerous homeopathic medicines that are available and legal in Europe but not in the United States.

* next to the name of a medicine indicates that this substance is available only by prescription from a veterinary physician or another doctor who can legally prescribe drugs. (Medical doctors can prescribe these drugs in every state, and naturopathic physicians can prescribe them in approximately 10 states.)

** next to the name of a medicine indicates that this substance is not available at all to any licensed or unlicensed person in the U.S. A medicine is not legal here either because it has not been formally tested and accepted by the Homeopathic Pharmacopeia Convention of the United States, or because the original ingredient is an FDA-controlled substance, even in the homeopathic infinitesimal dose, as is the case with **Opium.**

Resources for Veterinary Homeopathy

Veterinary Organization
American Holistic Veterinary Association
2214 Old Emmorton Road
Bel Air, MD. 21014

Homeopathic Organizations
National Center for Homeopathy
801 N. Fairfax #316
Alexandria, VA. 22314

International Foundation for Homeopathy
2366 Eastlake Ave. E.
Seattle, WA. 98104

Source of Books, Tapes, and Medicines
Homeopathic Educational Services
2124 Kittredge St.
Berkeley, CA. 94704

Courses in Veterinary Homeopathy
Richard Pitcairn, D.V.M., Ph.D.
1283 Lincoln St.
Eugene, OR. 97401

An Annotated Bibliography of Homeopathic Veterinary Books

Homeopathy in Veterinary Practice. K.J. Biddis. An excellent *materia medica*, preceded by a full, commonsense approach to casetaking and prescribing. It is followed by a therapeutic index, and it includes a chapter by the reknowned English homeopath G. MacLeod on "The Treatment of Goats".

Homeopathic Treatment of Small Animals. C. Day. Deals with dogs, cats, rats, mice, guinea pigs, hamsters, birds. Problems of the young and old, mental problems, common potency levels. A valuable materia medica, how to prescribe, use in surgery.

Cats: Homeopathic Remedies. George MacLeod. A sound introduction to remedy selection, nosodes and oral vaccines, and a full materia medica. Dr. MacLeod gives separate chapters on diseases of the alimentary system, respiratory system, lungs, nervous system, cardiovascular system, urinary tract, reproductive system, ear, eye, circulatory system, allergic conditions, muscles, skeletal system, eczemas, wounds, parasites, and various disease states such as leukemia, enteritis, and viral diseases.

Dogs: Homoeopathic Remedies. George MacLeod. This comprehensive book lists of the medicines for the various diseases that affect the different systems of the dog's body. Without oversimplifying, MacLeod describes several medicines to consider for each condition and recommends a specific potency.

Natural Health for Cats and Dogs. Richard Pitcairn, DVM, PhD, and Susan Pitcairn. More than just a book on using homeopathic medicines to treat cats and dogs, this book describes various natural therapies. It provides information on treating specific conditions and well as general information on good hygiene and preventive medicine.

Introductory Homeopathic Books

Everybody's Guide to Homeopathic Medicines. Dr. Stephen Cummings and Dana Ullman, Los Angeles, Jeremy Tarcher, 1991.

Homeopathic Medicine at Home. Dr. Maesimund Panos and Jane Heimlich, Los Angeles, Jeremy Tarcher, 1980.

Homeopathy: An Illustrated Guide. Sarah Richardson, New York, Crown, 1989.

Discovering Homeopathy: Medicine for the 21st Century. Dana Ullman. Berkeley, North Atlantic Books, 1991.

The Science of Homeopathy. George Vithoulkas. New York, Grove, 1980.